They Played for the Love of the Game

They Played for the Love of the Game

UNTOLD STORIES OF
BLACK BASEBALL IN MINNESOTA

Frank M. White

Foreword by DAVE WINFIELD

MINNESOTA
HISTORICAL
SOCIETY PRESS

CLEAN
WATER
LAND &
LEGACY
AMENDMENT

The Ramsey County Historical Society (RCHS) received a grant from the Arts and Cultural Heritage Fund that partially supported the development of this manuscript. Therefore RCHS and I wish to acknowledge that this project has been made possible, in part, by the Arts and Cultural Heritage Fund through the vote of Minnesotans on November 4, 2008. Administered by the Minnesota Historical Society.

Unless otherwise noted, photographs are provided courtesy of the author's collection.

Front cover: photograph from Minnesota Historical Society collections.
Back cover: top photograph from Minnesota Historical Society collections; bottom photograph courtesy of Sylvester Davis and Bob Rynda; jersey and cap from the author's collection, photographed by Jim Castle.

www.mnhspress.org

The Minnesota Historical Society Press is a member of the Association of American University Presses.

Manufactured in the United States of America

10 9 8 7 6 5 4 3 2 1

♾ The paper used in this publication meets the minimum requirements of the American National Standard for Information Sciences—Permanence for Printed Library Materials, ANSI Z39.48–1984.

International Standard Book Number
ISBN: 978-1-68134-004-3 (paper)
ISBN: 978-1-68134-005-0 (e-book)

Library of Congress Cataloging-in-Publication Data available upon request.

This and other Minnesota Historical Society Press books are available from popular e-book vendors.

To my father, his fellow ballplayers,
and others who loved the game of baseball
but whose stories are yet to be told.

Contents

Foreword by Dave Winfield ix

Preface and Acknowledgments xi

Foreword

by Dave Winfield

HAVE YOU EVER HAD ANYONE TELL YOU, "Once your mind has been expanded, it never goes back to its original size"? In this case, when you learn about history so close to yourself, you gain a completely new perspective on life, where you are from, and, in my case, your career.

Coming from the great state of Minnesota, I crafted what became a Hall of Fame career in professional baseball, spending more than two decades in Major League Baseball. After cutting, raking, and lining ball fields and playing the sandlots, playgrounds, alleys, and stadiums all across the state, I made it through youth baseball, high school, Attucks Brooks American Legion, the University of Minnesota, and later the Minnesota Twins. It was not a straight or easy road, but I learned that my path was much easier than my predecessors'.

I credit coaches, neighbors, family members, and many others for their unwavering support of my career and the teams my brother Steve and I played for. But equally as important, I tip my hat with admiration and respect to all those ballplayers presented in this volume. They preceded me, and they carried the same love of the game which, as I said in my Hall of Fame induction speech in 2001, is the "best game of all."

Preface and Acknowledgments

MY GOAL IN WRITING THIS HISTORY of black baseball in Minnesota is to share my personal journey around the sport, a journey that began with my earliest memories of watching my father, Louis "Pud" White II, play the great games of baseball and fast-pitch softball.

At those games in the 1950s at Como Park Field #1, Sumner Field in Minneapolis, or Lexington Park (home of the old St. Paul Saints), I would sit and watch the guys play, always with an eye on my father—how he threw the ball, his stance at the plate, the excitement when he hit the ball. Seeing my father hit a home run or other "rope" (hard line drive) always thrilled me. "That's my dad!" I would say. His teammates would say, "Way to go, Lou" or "Nice hit, Pud." I wanted to see his teammates do well, too. I loved going to the ballpark to watch my father and his friends. I just absorbed it all; after all, I was with my father.

Probably my greatest memories are from the early spring months, snow still on the ground, me waiting for my father to come home. "Dad, can we play catch today?" Some days yes; some days no. "Panch," he would say—my nickname being Pancho—"not today." It was only many years later that I understood he just needed to relax after a full day of work. But I can still vividly picture those days when he said, "Okay, Panch": my father about thirty yards away while I stood next to the driveway on the west end of the lot where we lived on St. Anthony Avenue, a half block from the Ober Boys Club and its baseball field. I would watch my father throw the ball to me and then try to match his technique and style on my return. Sometimes he would sneak in "a little heat" on his throws, just to see my reaction. I wouldn't say anything to make him think that I couldn't handle it. I can't tell you how much those moments meant to me, just my father and me playing catch.

Later, when I was a junior in high school in 1962, I remember watching our old black-and-white TV and hearing something about Jackie Robinson being mentioned during a Dodgers game.

"You know who Jackie Robinson replaced at first base?" my father asked me.

"No," I replied.

"Your coach!"

What? "Who, Dad?" I asked.

"Your coach, Howie Schultz!"

My father explained that Schultz, himself a St. Paul native, had played for the Brooklyn Dodgers in the 1940s, as well as for the Minneapolis Lakers in the National Basketball Association during the early '50s. Wow! I was playing for a very special person, and a former professional basketball and baseball player. Unfortunately, I never knew how to bring up the subject with Howie; the time never seemed right. All these decades later, I regret never asking Howie about his time with Jackie Robinson, their spring training in Cuba in 1947, his helping Jackie learn to play first base—the same position I played for two years in high school.

When I was a young kid, I'd never heard of the Negro Leagues or the amazing black players from those teams, like Satchel Paige, Double Duty Radcliffe, Hilton Smith, or the great home run hitter and catcher Josh Gibson. I only knew of the major leaguers like Jackie Robinson, Roy Campanella, and Don Newcombe, and I had seen Charlie Neal play for the St. Paul Saints.

One time, in about 1959 or 1960, my father took me to a Hot Stove Banquet, a gathering of fans and some former players to talk baseball during the cold winter months of the off-season. At the time I didn't know why we went, but all these years later I now understand my father's connection to the sport and that he knew a lot of the old players who showed up. I got to meet Ted "Double Duty" Radcliffe, who shared some great baseball stories. As we were leaving, I asked, "Who was that, Dad?" My father explained that Radcliffe played in the Negro Leagues during the 1930s and '40s. He was an excellent talent who played both pitcher and catcher during his career. (Double Duty earned his nickname, courtesy of legendary sportswriter Damon Runyon, after catching for Satchel Paige in a shutout for the first game of a doubleheader in the 1932 Negro League World Series and then pitching a shutout himself in the second game.) Many years later, I saw two different interviews with local media featuring Double Duty and my father.

My father was an outstanding athlete and a very, very good baseball and, later, fast-pitch softball player. He was an outstanding catcher, and with his strong arm behind the plate, not many guys stole bases against him. Even more impressive was his hitting ability.

Growing up, I was always called "Little Lou" by my father's friends and people in the neighborhood. I played football, basketball, and baseball, and people had high expectations because I was "Pud's son." I remember feeling proud to have this connection to my father, but I also wanted my own identity. I'd sometimes think to myself, "My name is Frank." As I got older, I realized it was really an honor to have my talents linked to my father's.

In the late 1980s, the Minnesota Historical Society had an exhibit on black baseball in Minnesota. My father asked me to take him. What I learned at this event inspired me to take on the challenge of sharing the history of black baseball and the forgotten tales of the 1940s, '50s, and '60s. I was fascinated by the stories being told by men like Jimmy Griffin, LeRoy Hardeman, W. Harry Davis, Larry "Bubba" Brown, and my father. These were highly respected men in the African American community, especially Jim in St. Paul and Harry in Minneapolis, both important community leaders in their respective cities. LeRoy had been an outstanding athlete who played fast-pitch softball with my father back in the 1950s and '60s. Bubba, another great athlete, later shared many stories about playing against my father and others. I and other young black men looked up to these guys when we were growing up.

Retired black baseball players at an event at the Minnesota History Center in St. Paul: (back row, left to right) LeRoy Hardeman, Louis White, W. Harry Davis; (front row, left to right) Jimmy Griffin, Earl "Lefty" Evans, Lawrence "Bubba" Brown. Photo by Frank M. White

At the historical society event, these men talked at length about playing baseball, about the great local ballplayers of their day, and about the Negro League teams that came through the Twin Cities on barnstorming tours. Jimmy Robinson, who had known my father for many years and was active in the local African American sports community, said to me, "You know, they used to come and get your dad to play." "Who?" I asked. Jim said, "Those Negro League teams. They would ask your father to play with them." What? Wow! Really? Jim explained how good a player my father was. It made me feel so proud.

As my father and I drove home from the event, I shared with him what Jim had told me. I asked him why he never told me about how he used to play with the Negro League teams. He replied, "It wasn't important." Unbelievable! Oh, well: that was my father.

◆　　◆　　◆

I always loved playing sports, and baseball was the first game I learned. The first team I played for was at Front Recreation Center in St. Paul. I remember going out for the pee wee team when I was about nine years old. I remember the tryouts and practices and the day I made the team and received that royal blue baseball cap with an "F" on the front. I remember sitting, filled with nervous excitement, as the coach called out the names of the kids who would get a cap. Finally my name was called, and I couldn't wait to go home and show my father. "Dad, look! I made the team!" He gave a small smile like only my father could and said, "Good for you!" Like so many fathers from his generation, he wasn't going to make a large display of emotion—men were men—but for me, after watching my father play, I just wanted to be like him: a baseball player, at least in the summertime.

As kids, we cherished the game with each new day, meeting friends at the ball field to pick up where we left off the day before. If we didn't have enough players for a game, we'd play anyway, adding such rules as you were out if you hit the ball to rightfield, since we didn't have enough players to cover the whole field. We would play for hours, sometimes into the evening when you could hardly see the ball or until I heard Dad's whistle telling me it was time to come home for dinner.

Growing up, we didn't have much, so baseball equipment was at a premium. A baseball would be used until the cover started to tear, and then we would wrap it with tape and continue. Sometimes we would get cracked bats from my father's games; we would attempt to fix them with nails, tape, or both, and then it was off to the baseball diamond. One of my most exciting memories is getting a new glove for Christmas, and then waiting with anticipation for months before the weather was nice enough that I could use it. But you can bet I was oiling the glove each night, placing a ball in the pocket and then wrapping a belt or rope around it in order to make that great pocket so all my friends would be impressed.

◆　◆　◆

Another moment, years later, inspired me to follow this journey and learn more about the untold history of Minnesota's great black ballplayers. In the summer of 2004, my younger brother, Louis III, and I were traveling to Kansas City, Missouri, for business. During the six-hour drive, I shared with him how I had learned that our father played with and against the Negro League teams that barnstormed through the Twin Cities, playing at Lexington and Nicollet Parks. I told him how Jimmy Robinson said our father was a great ballplayer and how Dad later said it "wasn't important." My brother understood how Dad was.

As we arrived in Kansas City, my cell phone rang. It was my sister Linda. She told me that Dad's surgery had been moved up to the next morning. I told Louis, and he wanted to turn around and head back home to be with our father.

I reminded him that we both had business to take care of in Kansas City, and I had promised Dad that I would bring him something from the Negro Leagues Baseball Museum. I set a plan to go to our meetings the next morning, visit the museum, and return home in time to see Dad when he was out of surgery and in recovery.

After attending to our business the next day, Louis and I headed to the museum. Little did we know what was in store for us.

As we walked through the museum, my phone rang. It was Steve Winfield, Dave Winfield's brother; I consider both Steve and David to be my brothers through our extended families. He asked where I was, and I told him. Steve said that Dave had signed a ball that was supposed to be on display at the museum. I hadn't seen it, so we went into the souvenir shop to find out. I told the gentleman there that my brother had signed a ball but I didn't see it on display anywhere. He asked, "Who's your brother?" I said, "Dave Winfield." He got excited and grabbed a camera and asked us to take a picture in the museum next to one of the statues. Of course, it had to be the legendary Negro Leagues catcher Josh Gibson, since our father had been a catcher, too.

A few minutes later, this gentleman saw Buck O'Neil in the lobby and called to him—"Mr. O'Neil, Mr. O'Neil"—and grabbed a couple of photos for Buck to autograph. He introduced us, saying "These guys claim to be Winfields." I explained, "No, we're Whites, but we're extended family members." I asked Buck if he would sign two more pictures, one each for Dave and Steve. I went back into the shop to get the photos.

Me, Steve Winfield, Jim Griffin (in the background), Jimmy Lee, Dave Winfield, and Bill Peter-
son, in 1973, during Dave's first season with the San Diego Padres. He was presented with the
Lions Club award for outstanding amateur athlete of St. Paul at the Attucks Brooks American
Legion hall.

When I rejoined the group, my brother was telling Buck that our father played against Negro League teams in Minnesota. Buck asked our father's name, and when my brother replied, "Louis White," Buck's eyes widened, and he said, "Your dad is Lou White?" I couldn't believe it. The great Buck O'Neil knew my dad. Buck asked if he was still alive, and we explained that he was having surgery as we spoke. Buck said to make sure to say "hello" for him.

After I treated my brother to lunch at the Peachtree restaurant (the best in KC!), we returned to St. Paul and went directly to the hospital. My sisters said Dad couldn't talk yet because of the surgery but he was in the recovery room. I went in to see my father, and he was lying there quietly. I leaned over and said that Buck O'Neil told me to tell him "hello." My dad's eyes grew large as he acknowledged the greeting.

We returned to Kansas City and the museum later in the spring with my father and other family members for a visit with Buck O'Neil. The meeting was arranged by Bob Kendrick, a friend of Buck's who was the marketing director of the Negro Leagues Baseball Museum and later its president.

Kwame McDonald, a longtime civil rights activist who also had a cable show in St. Paul called *Sports Rap*, asked if he could join us. He would do an interview with Buck and my father, and I would be the cameraman. The staff at the Negro Leagues Baseball Museum made all the arrangements. The interview took place in front of the Satchel Paige statue in the center of the museum. People who were visiting the museum would stop and listen. Most of them also went into the souvenir shop to buy a ball or book or other item to be autographed.

Buck O'Neil was entertaining, knowledgeable, and gracious to everyone, especially my father. The original interview was about forty-five minutes and was aired on the St. Paul Neighborhood Network (SPNN) on *Sports Rap*.

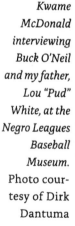

Kwame McDonald interviewing Buck O'Neil and my father, Lou "Pud" White, at the Negro Leagues Baseball Museum. Photo courtesy of Dirk Dantuma

After the interview, people lined up to ask Buck for an autograph. Buck signed whatever was placed in front of him, and then he would pass it to my father to sign as well. A young boy next to me was excited as he looked at me behind the camera. "Do you know who these guys are?" he asked. "They're Negro League players!" His mother explained that her son knew a lot about the Negro Leagues—this young boy about ten years old happened to be white. His excitement was inspiring.

When we got back to the motel to relax after the museum, the staff approached my father and asked for a picture of him for their "wall of fame."

The next morning, I took Dad to Leavenworth, Kansas, where his mother was born and had lived before coming to Minnesota. During the drive, I turned to my father and said, "Dad, you're really getting some props. How does that feel?" He replied, "Panch, I didn't think I would get another chance to take a trip with the family." My father had found out after the surgery that his illness was terminal. I thought to myself, "C'mon man, you're killing me." But inside my heart I knew how he really felt, and it made me proud to have been called "Little Lou."

◆　　◆　　◆

Learning more about this small thread connecting me to baseball history helped to plant the seed that led me to work with the Ramsey County Historical Society in 2009 and 2010 to create the exhibit "They Played for the Love of the Game: Adding to the Legacy of Minnesota Black Baseball."

In addition to personal experiences with my father and inspiring moments like seeing the young boy at the Negro Leagues Baseball Museum, two previous books that attempted to tell the story of black baseball in Minnesota pushed me to explore the subject further. The first was *Swinging for the Fences*, edited by Steven R. Hoffbeck and published in 2005. Todd Peterson's *Early Black Baseball in Minnesota*, published in 2010, was another vital resource.

I knew that Kwame McDonald contributed two chapters to Hoffbeck's collection, and when I first saw the book with Dave Winfield's photo on the cover, I was excited to read it. But I ended up being disappointed because it discussed only one local player that I remember hearing about from the early years of black baseball, Maceo Breedlove. The book focused more on the big stars who came through Minnesota. I mean no disrespect to the editor, but as someone who saw many games between the Twin City Colored Giants and others, I was looking for some recognition of the many men who played for local teams, including my father.

As I began my journey to tell the deeper stories of these players and teams, I came to understand the challenges in researching black baseball in Minnesota. If you're writing about the Minneapolis Millers or the St. Paul Saints or the Minnesota Twins, there's plenty of documentation available. But attempting to offer a complete history of black baseball is nearly impossible. The materials are just not widely available.

I was fortunate to be able to consult these two books whose authors did a very good job of telling their vision and part of the story. Their work helped inspire me to focus on the stories from the 1940s through the 1960s. To provide a fuller picture, I included the early eras as well, and my research helped to uncover some additional information and identification of players, teams, and their travels.

Throughout my research and interviews with people who knew our family, I've learned a great deal about black baseball and African American history in Minnesota. I still get excited when I find out something new. I also have an emptiness knowing that it's taken so long for me to find out about these players—fathers and heroes to many—that history has forgotten.

Is this the complete story of black baseball in Minnesota? No, but it contributes to understanding the experiences of African Americans who played the great game while living, every day, with the indignities of Jim Crow and the denial of opportunities. Their stories are a part of our history in Minnesota. Segregation in baseball, in where you could live, in where you could eat—this reality wasn't only in the South. It happened here in the upper Midwest as well. My hope is that understanding this history will help us to learn to treat each other with love and respect as we share this time and space in Minnesota.

After so many decades as a baseball fan, I've come to appreciate the groundbreaking African Americans who played under such difficult circumstances, whether in the Negro Leagues or close to home in Minnesota. Baseball was segregated in the North Star State for generations, and many of the state's greatest ballplayers have gone unrecognized and remain unknown today. As in much of black history, documentation is sparse, but my goal is to tell as much as I can about the history of Minnesota black baseball, its players, and the challenges they faced. Come with me as I turn back the pages to a time long since passed. Batter up!

◆　◆　◆

Writing this book has been one of the most difficult tasks I've undertaken. For helping me accomplish it, I want to thank Mollie Spillman, John Lindley, Bill Peterson, and Steve Winfield, each of whom inspired me at different times in the process.

I was always eager to listen whenever guys like Johnny Cotton, Larry "Bubba" Brown, Ken Christian, James Millsap, and Jim Robinson—all local sports pioneers—shared their recollections of the great ballplayers they watched back in the 1940s and '50s.

Jim Robinson, in particular, has been an outstanding resource, sharing many stories about my father and others as well as offering insights into what life was like for black folks in Minnesota during those days. A long-time friend of mine, Jim had been a talented athlete at Mechanic Arts High School and served as the bat boy for the Twin City Colored Giants team my father played for. Jim has also become a community leader in St. Paul, one of our first African American basketball officials; he worked in the Big Ten and eventually became the supervisor of basketball officials for the Minnesota State High School League.

To my wife, Lisa: thank you for keeping me on task, or at least attempting to.

To my father and mother, whose inspiration every day has given me the strength to stand up and be counted. I am proud of the values they instilled in me and my siblings. I think back and wonder how they made it all work—we didn't have much—and I love them for what they gave us and the sacrifices they made to raise our family.

Special Acknowledgment

I want to thank Ramsey County Historical Society and the members of its staff for inspiring me to venture on this journey of writing a book and further sharing the untold story of African Americans playing baseball in Minnesota.

The beginning surely was our partnership in curating my exhibit, "They Played for the Love of the Game: Adding to the Legacy of Minnesota Black Baseball." The next part of the journey was writing an article for *Ramsey County History*, the quarterly history magazine that RCHS publishes. My article in the spring 2010 issue was very well received and further inspired me to continue to share the story.

I especially would like to thank Mollie Spillman, curator/archivist, and John M. Lindley, editor, for their continued support and the resources they provided as I sought to write this story, particularly during those times when I was challenged or frustrated by the lack of historical documentation. Without their push and taking time to listen, I'm not sure where this project would have ended.

They Played for the Love of the Game

·1·
Beginnings
Minnesota Black Baseball
in the Nineteenth Century

THE HISTORY OF AFRICAN AMERICANS IN MINNESOTA goes back to the earliest Euro-American settlements in the area. Black men and women, both free and enslaved, lived at Fort Snelling, which was the foundation of what would become the state of Minnesota. This military outpost was built at the confluence of the Minnesota and Mississippi Rivers between 1820 and 1825.

Although slavery was illegal in the territory according to U.S. law, historians estimate that, during the 1820s and '30s, anywhere from fifteen to thirty enslaved African Americans lived and worked at the fort at any given time. Among the territory's prominent African Americans in the years before statehood was James Thompson, who was brought to Fort Snelling from Virginia by way of Kentucky as a slave in 1827. About a decade later, Reverend Alfred Brunson paid for Thompson's freedom, and he became a Dakota interpreter for the Methodist mission. Thompson later was an early resident of the burgeoning city of St. Paul, then known as Pig's Eye. Dred and Harriet Scott—whose infamous Supreme Court case, *Scott v. Sandford* (1857), would be a landmark constitutional decision and bring the nation closer to Civil War—lived as slaves at Fort Snelling in the 1830s.

In the years following the Civil War, more African Americans settled in Minnesota. In 1866, a group known as the "Pilgrims," who had first arrived in St. Paul as fugitive slaves in 1863, formally established a church at 732

Dred and Harriet Scott, depicted in Century Magazine, *June 1887.* Library of Congress Prints and Photographs Division

West Central Avenue in St. Paul. Now on the National Register of Historic Places, Pilgrim Baptist Church is Minnesota's oldest black church and has served the community for 150 years.

The immediate postwar years were also a boom period for America's national pastime. While baseball had been growing in popularity on the East Coast since the 1840s, other regions of the country were exposed to the sport during the Civil War. Games were sometimes played between regiments from different states as a form of exercise and R & R during wartime, and soldiers returning to Minnesota brought the sport home with them.

The nation's first organized baseball league, the National Association of Base Ball Players, had been established in 1857 with fourteen member clubs, all from the New York City area. A decade later, at the 1867 annual convention, the association boasted membership in the hundreds, with teams located in all corners of the country.

It was also at this time that organized baseball entered a dark period

GRAND
MASS MEETING
OF THE
COLORED PEOPLE OF MINNESOTA,
JANUARY 1st, 1869.

COME ONE! COME ALL!

There will be held in the city of St. Paul, on January 1st, 1869, at noon, in Ingersoll's Hall, A GRAND

MASS MEETING OF THE COLORED PEOPLE

Of the whole State, to celebrate the

EMANCIPATION

Of Four Million Slaves, and to express our gratitude for the bestowal of the elective franchise to the Colored People of this State, and to perfect a State Organization of the Sons of Freedom.

Gov. Wm. R. Marshall,
Dr. J. H. Stewart, Mayor of St. Paul,
Hon. I. Donnelly,
Hon. Morton S. Wilkinson,
Lt.-Gov. Thos. H. Armstrong,
Gen. Levi Nutting,

And others, are expected to be present and address the people. In the evening, after the meeting, there will be served a Splendid SUPPER, tickets to which will be distributed during the afternoon by the Committee.

NO CHARGE FOR ANYTHING.

Friends from abroad come and help us rejoice. Let there be a grand turn out.

MAURICE JERNIGAN,
ROBERT HICKMAN,
THOS. A. JACKSON,
GEO. B. WILLIAMS,
JOHN. A. JACKSON,
DAVID EDWARDS,
GEORGE DENNIS,
CLIFTON MONROE,
EDMOND JAMES,

ENASE WALKER,
PHELAN COMBS, Sr.,
JOHN H. MOFFIT,
HENRY TROTTER,
WM. SINGLETON,
ROBERT BANKS,
GEO. ANDERSON,
ADDISON DRAKE,
HENRY GILES,

Committee.

(St. Paul Press.)

Poster announcing a celebration of emancipation in St. Paul, January 1, 1869. Minnesota Historical Society Collections

from which it would not emerge for eighty years. At the annual convention in December 1867, the National Association agreed to ban "any club which may be composed of one or more colored persons." This announcement came just two years after the Thirteenth Amendment to the U.S. Constitution outlawed slavery and just a year before ratification of the Fourteenth Amendment granted full citizenship to African Americans.

When the National League of Professional Base Ball Clubs—better known as, simply, the National League—was formed in February 1876, it honored the precedent established by its predecessor: black ballplayers were excluded from all National League clubs.

At first, not all leagues followed suit, and during the last quarter of the nineteenth century as many as seventy African Americans played on professional baseball teams. In 1884, brothers Fleet and Weldy Walker played for the Toledo Blue Stockings of the American Association, a major league rival of the National League. In his seminal *History of Colored Base Ball,* Sol White called 1887 a "banner year for colored talent in the white leagues," with "no less than twenty colored ball players scattered among the different smaller leagues of the country." During that off-season, however, all organized leagues "drew the color line, or had a clause inserted in their constitutions limiting the number of colored players to be employed by each club."

One of the most important figures in the early history of blacks in baseball had a connection to the game in Minnesota. Bud Fowler, often credited as the first African American player in organized baseball, spent time with the Stillwater ball club of the Northwestern League in 1884.

Fowler was born on March 16, 1858, in upstate New York and lived his early life in Cooperstown, later the home of the National Baseball Hall of Fame. Beginning in his late teen years, he pitched for various semi-professional baseball clubs. In 1878, he appeared briefly with the Live Oaks of Lynn, Massachusetts, in the International Association. It was this experience that first brought him into the fold of organized professional baseball.

Stillwater, Minnesota, became a part of the professional baseball circuit when the Northwestern League expanded to twelve teams in 1884.

The Northwestern League was considered a premier minor league at the time. Fowler went to Stillwater to be the team's pitcher.

Signing Fowler proved to be one of the few positives for Stillwater that year. Fowler led all Stillwater pitchers with seven wins, and he was also the team's top hitter, with a .302 average. Following a Stillwater victory in Terre Haute, Indiana, the *Terre Haute Evening Gazette* proclaimed, "Fowler, the colored player who twirled the sphere for the visitors, pitched a fine game and batted well." Stillwater posted a dismal 21–45 record overall, however, and the team folded in August due to financial struggles. Fowler next landed in the Western League to play for a team in Keokuk, Iowa, where he would be one of the best and most popular players in 1885.

It wasn't long before this window of opportunity for African Americans in organized baseball would be closed. In 1887, Fowler was playing for the Binghamton (NY) Crickets of the International League, another top minor league and feeder circuit for the majors. Even though he had an impressive .350 batting average with 42 runs and 23 stolen bases in 34 games, Fowler's teammates refused to take the field alongside him for a game. He was released by Binghamton shortly thereafter.

Perhaps the biggest blow that led to the complete shift to segregated baseball came in July of that year, when Cap Anson's Chicago White Stockings of the National League were scheduled to play an exhibition game against the Newark Giants of the International League. The Giants roster included African Americans Fleet Walker and George Stovey. Anson refused to allow his team to take the field if Walker and Stovey played, and so Newark benched the two players. Later that same day, International League owners voted to allow "no more contracts with colored men," citing the "hazards" imposed by such athletes.

Bud Fowler continued to play professional baseball until 1895. Over his career, he suited up for more than a dozen integrated teams in a variety of minor leagues—from New Hampshire to New Mexico—but never in a major league. After 1895, Fowler primarily played for all-black teams, including the legendary barnstorming Page Fence Giants of Michigan, which he organized and managed himself.

By the end of the nineteenth century, all major and minor leagues that constituted "organized baseball," led by the National League and American Association, had signed on to the so-called gentleman's agreement banning African Americans. By agreeing to withhold contracts to black players, the baseball owners reflected the continuing momentum toward formal segregation in American society, an approach that was upheld by the U.S. Supreme Court in the *Plessy v. Ferguson* case of 1896, which dealt with segregated railroad facilities. The decision argued that as long as "separate but equal" accommodations were provided, then segregation did not constitute discrimination. In practice, however, many states, particularly in the South, took *Plessy v. Ferguson* as a blanket approval for enacting restrictive laws, generally known as Jim Crow laws, to further ensure second-class status for African Americans in all walks of life.

◆　◆　◆

Why Keokuk?

ONE THING that has always fascinated me is the question, "why here?" Why is a particular town located here? Why would someone want to live here? This curiosity has regularly come to the fore in my research about black baseball players in the late nineteenth and early twentieth centuries, when individuals ended up playing in seemingly random locations that, one would think, would not have carried much attraction for African Americans. I was especially intrigued to learn that Bud Fowler played with a team from Keokuk, Iowa, in 1885.

During a short weekend trip with my wife along the Mississippi River to McGregor, Iowa, I came upon a sign that pointed to Keokuk, and I remembered Fowler, which sparked me to do a little research about this city. Known as the Gate City, Keokuk is located at the junction of the Mississippi and Des Moines Rivers, in the far southeastern corner of Iowa, just across the border from Missouri and Illinois. A small African American community had developed there in the latter half of the nineteenth century, and its members sought to attract more black residents to this rural Iowa city.

A letter to the editor in St. Paul's *Western Appeal* newspaper on July 30, 1887, included promotional copy about Keokuk:

> Your many readers will doubtless accept with interest and pleasure a few items from the Gate City of Iowa. This is the fifth city in size in the state, and is beautifully located on the banks of the broad Mississippi and the placid Des Moines rivers. Our people number nearly three thousand. The majority own their own cosy homes and make a fair living. We have one of the best school systems in the county, and there is no reason why any of our young people should grow up in ignorance. We boast of four colored churches, two Baptist, one A. M. E. and an Episcopal, the latter has been recently organized, but it is progressing so rapidly and creating so much interest among its attendants that it bids fair to become the church among our people.

Perhaps it was a notice such as this that convinced Fowler, a native of New York State, that playing baseball in Keokuk, Iowa, was an opportunity he could not pass up. ●

Even before the overt ban of African Americans from organized professional baseball, all-black teams had been forming and playing against each other as well as against all-white teams as early as 1860, mainly on the East Coast and in the mid-Atlantic states. According to Todd Peterson, in his book *Early Black Baseball in Minnesota*, "African Americans took up the national pastime while imprisoned in the South during the 18th century, with the first organized black teams emerging just prior to the Civil War."

In Minnesota, African Americans were playing on integrated baseball teams by the early 1870s. It is difficult to document who was the first African American to play baseball in Minnesota, but there are accounts of some of those early players.

The 1885 Keokuk baseball club, featuring Bud Fowler (back row, center)

Prince Honeycutt, Minnesota's presumed first black baseball player, standing outside his barbershop in Fergus Falls. Otter Tail County Historical Society

Author Steven Hoffbeck cites Prince Honeycutt as the first African American baseball player on record in Minnesota. Originally from Tennessee, Honeycutt arrived in Fergus Falls in 1872, becoming the first black resident of that western Minnesota town. He operated a barbershop and, a year after his arrival, helped form the Fergus Falls North Stars baseball club, later known as the Musculars. As a young teenager during the Civil War, Honeycutt had served as a "mess boy" for a Union soldier, whom he eventually followed to Fergus Falls. It may have been during his time with the Union Army that Honeycutt was first exposed to the game of baseball.

As the number of black teams in Minnesota increased in the latter years of the nineteenth century, rivalries developed between teams from Minneapolis and teams from St. Paul. Building on a sense of competition between the cities that is almost as old as the state itself, these rivalries would extend to baseball at every level, whether high school, youth and adult, or the St. Paul Saints and Minneapolis Millers of the American Association.

One of the earliest recorded games between black baseball teams in Minnesota was in August 1876 between the Minneapolis Unions and the St. Paul Blue Stars, which the Unions won 37–28. A few weeks later, the St. Paul club blanked the Minneapolis team 23–0, but according to Hoffbeck, the Unions left the field after the third inning, claiming that the Blue Stars had unfairly used three professional players from Chicago.

It wasn't the first time a Minnesota team recruited a player for an important game, and for sure it wouldn't be the last. The previous September, the Winona Clippers brought in W. W. Fisher of the Chicago Uniques to help them defeat the St. Paul Red Caps, 24–22, in the state championship.

The growing popularity of the sport within the Twin Cities' African American community is evident in the regular announcements that appeared in the local black press connecting baseball with larger social and recreational activities. On July 16, 1887, the *Western Appeal* newspaper ran an announcement for the Union Picnic at Excelsior Park in Minnetonka. Among the activities and events were various speakers, music, boating, swimming, fishing, a "Grand Parade" headed by the Minneapolis Central Band, and "A Game of Ball . . . For the Championship of the Northwest."

The St. Paul Quicksteps had issued a challenge to "any colored baseball club" in the area to take them on in a championship series. The Minneapolis Brown Stockings accepted the call, and the two teams played in Excelsior on August 1. The Quicksteps were victorious and laid claim to the title of champions of the Northwest. No score was given in the newspaper report.

The August 13 edition of the *Western Appeal* noted that the Quicksteps "have accepted a challenge from the Fort Snelling club and will play the game Monday the 15th. . . . The game will take place on the Snelling grounds. All parties who wish to witness the game can go in the busses which have been chartered for the occasion upon application to Messrs. C. A. Lett or W. D. Carter." As indicated in the accompanying listing of the Quicksteps' lineup, Lett was the team captain and Carter the manager.

St. Paul Quicksteps Lineup

W. D. Carter, MANAGER
Jas. Duke, P
T. H. Long, C
W. H. Brown, 1B
C. A. Lett, 2B AND CAPTAIN
C. Wilkins, 3B
H. F. Newton, LF
A. Leboo, CF
W. H. Springer, RF
H. W. Fairfax, SS
A. A. Cotton, SUBSTITUTE

The item concluded with the note: "The clubs are very anxious to have as many present, and all are invited. There is no charge to witness the game."

The paper reported a week later that the Quicksteps were victorious by a score of 11–5. The game was followed by a "dress parade," courtesy of the officers at Fort Snelling, "who made things very pleasant for all."

The Quicksteps' next match was in Shakopee, against the Shakopee Reserves, and they were defeated handily, 23–4. An announcement in the *Western Appeal* prior to the game on August 20 announced that the Quicksteps were to "leave the Union Depot at 8:30, and all who wish to go are invited. Fare for round trip $1.40."

Although there is very little documentation on Minnesota's black baseball teams of the late 1800s, the *Western Appeal* newspaper played an important role in sharing information with the African American community about local social events, including sports. On June 9, 1888, the paper reported that the "Little Diamond baseball club wishes to challenge any Colored club in Minnesota to play them. All correspondence to be addressed to John Samuels (captain) 256—6th Avenue So."

More and more team names appear in the pages of the black press through the final decade of the century. The June 12, 1897, edition of the *Appeal* announced that the "Douglass Base Ball Club has been reorganized and would like a game for every Saturday during the summer. The first game will be played Saturday, June 19 with the Adler Kids at Aurora Park." The Douglass manager was given as C. M. Tibes, who, the article continued, "hopes to present the following team: A. M. Lee-p, C. H. Miller-c, Willie Williams-1st b, Geo. Bailey-2nd b, Harry Franklin-3rd b, Andrew Combs-ss, R. Farr-lf, John Kelley-cf, Willie Greene-rf."

Thanks to the various African American newspapers operating in Minneapolis and St. Paul, folks in the Twin Cities not only were kept well informed of happenings around town but also were well connected to what was going on in the rest of the country. The railroads provided another vital link, employing many African American men who traveled back and forth to Chicago and other larger cities. In the July 2, 1887, issue of the *Western Appeal*, no fewer than six different ads promoted travel to Chicago, St. Louis, Kansas City, Des Moines, and cities beyond. These connections were key to the region's growth and of great benefit for baseball as well, as Twin Citians were able to learn about and recruit black players from Chicago and elsewhere.

One of the key people involved in building connections with other black communities was John Quincy Adams. Adams arrived in St. Paul from Louisville, Kentucky, in August 1886 to take the job of assistant editor of the *Western Appeal* newspaper, which had begun publication the previous year. He was promoted to editor in 1887 and, shortly thereafter, became the paper's sole proprietor as well. Adams would spearhead the paper's growth and success over the next thirty-five years.

Adams opened an additional office in Minneapolis and, in January 1888, another one in Chicago, challenging that city's other black newspapers. By December of 1888, the *Western Appeal* claimed to be

John Quincy Adams, circa 1892. Minnesota Historical Society Collections

Chicago's leading black newspaper. Over subsequent years, Adams established branch offices in Louisville, St. Louis, Dallas, and Washington, DC. Dropping the word "Western" from its name in 1889, the *Appeal* also carried bylines from Milwaukee, Des Moines, and Denver from time to time. It billed itself a "National Afro-American Newspaper."

The African American press played a vital role in black communities throughout the United States during this period. As David V. Taylor wrote in his 1973 article "John Quincy Adams: St. Paul Editor and Black Leader" for *Minnesota History* magazine, "Since its inception the Black press has been at the focal point of every issue concerning the self-determination of Black people and has provided an open arena where the battle for recognition could be successfully waged. By stressing racial pride it forged a sense of ethnic solidarity and group cohesion which united the Black community."

The success of John Q. Adams and his newspaper, and his role as a civic leader in St. Paul and beyond, came at a time of considerable change and challenges. In the 1880s, African Americans in Minnesota enjoyed many privileges of citizenship unknown to their southern brethren. African American males could exercise the right to vote and hold public office, and blacks in Minnesota were accorded a greater degree of mobility and social interaction, in general, with whites than southern blacks were.

State civil rights laws had been passed in 1865 and 1885. The first law guaranteed full male suffrage (with the exception of full-blooded Indians who refused to accept "civilization"). The law of 1885 guaranteed equal rights to all citizens regardless of "nativity, race, color or persuasion, religious or political." The rights included full and equal enjoyment of all public accommodations, conveyances, facilities, and so on.

A subsequent act, signed into law by Governor John Lind in 1899, strengthened the equal protection elements of the 1885 law with regard to the enjoyment of public accommodations, particularly places of business and amusement. Introduced by J. Frank Wheaton, the first African American to serve in the Minnesota state legislature (and the last until 1972), the law prohibited the exclusion of persons, "on account of race or color, from full and equal enjoyment of any accommodation, advantage,

or privilege furnished by public conveyances, theaters, or other places
of amusement, or by hotels, barbershops, saloons, restaurants, or other
places of refreshment, entertainment, or accommodation."

But even while state laws prohibited Jim Crow policies and protected
the voting rights of African American males, and in spite of noteworthy
progress in business enterprise, landhold-
ings, education, and literacy in the late
1800s, African Americans in Minnesota
nevertheless faced much outright discrimination and began to see the encroachment
of de facto segregation.

J. Frank Wheaton, circa 1899.
Minnesota Historical
Society Collections

•2•
The Early Twentieth Century
Black Baseball:
Gophers and Keystones

DESPITE THE CONTINUING SPREAD of Jim Crow laws in both the South and the North, the dawn of the twentieth century brought the promise of hope for many African Americans. The Great Migration was beginning, and people of all colors were hoping to take advantage of new opportunities within the industrial growth of northern cities. Blacks, in particular, were seeking a road to the promised land.

However, the North was not always the land of milk and honey. The following story appeared in the *St. Paul Globe* on September 1, 1903:

Waterloo is "Lily White"

Iowa Town Drives Away the Entire Negro Population

WATERLOO, IOWA. AUG. 31—An "All White City" is the motto adopted for Waterloo, and the citizens are bending their energies to the end that this motto is lived to. This means not only that negroes are not wanted as residents, but that they will not be tolerated here. The "reform" began but a few weeks ago, but so vigorously has it been carried forward that today one can search the city over and in all its borders he will not be able to find a man, woman or child with a black skin. Those who were here, numbering a dozen families or so, were notified that their presence was no longer desired. No violence was resorted to and none was threatened, but the colored people knew what the warning meant, and in less than a week after the edict had gone forth there was an exodus of the black folks, which has been continued until they have all departed. . . .

The matter was recently brought to a climax when two negro baseball teams were brought to the city. Waterloo has a baseball nine of white players, and in order to attract players worthy to contest the sport with them, the negroes, who had proven their prowess at other places, were invited for a series of games.

Then the trouble began. These dusky players, because they were associated with white men in their sport, assumed an air of equality with their competitors. They were really good ball players, and their work on the diamond made them heroes in the eyes of many susceptible people, especially young white girls. They were not slow to take what advantages they could, socially, of this, and parents of several of the girls were suddenly aroused to the condition of affairs.

No open action was taken then, and no demonstration was made against the players, but after the colored ball team had departed it became understood that a second invitation for them to visit Waterloo would be resented.

The matter took on such a serious turn that one of the daily papers of the city began a crusade against the negro and freely advised those in the city that their presence would not be longer tolerated, that Waterloo was to be a white man's town, and that a quiet departure would save the adoption of harsh measures for their removal.

Such experiences and troubles were not uncommon, in towns large and small, both northern and southern. Even as some African Americans were making advances politically and in business, the message remained clear: "you better know your place."

Still, the hope of jobs, property, and a better way of life led many southern blacks to move north, and some northern cities encouraged this migration. One of Minneapolis's black newspapers proclaimed in 1899, "There is not another city in the Union where white people are so friendly disposed toward African Americans."

The newspaper's claims notwithstanding, black people in the Twin Cities faced many obstacles to finding employment, housing, and education. Job discrimination, school segregation, and open hostility from white citizens were everyday realities. The African Americans who settled in the Twin Cities were mostly poor and working class. The best jobs available to the men tended to be with local hotels, restaurants, or railroads as janitors, waiters, and porters, while black women could mostly only find work as domestic servants or laundresses.

A black professional class was emerging in Minnesota, however, and

The choir of St. Peter Claver Church in St. Paul, circa 1901; the church was an important corner-stone of the city's African American community. Minnesota Historical Society Collections

African Americans were pursuing education to lead them on the road to a better life. The first black students at the University of Minnesota were few in number but strong in aspiration.

In 1882, Andrew Hilyer became the first African American to graduate from the University of Minnesota. Hilyer, who was born a slave in Georgia in 1858, later earned law degrees from Howard University and would work for several federal agencies in Washington, DC. He was also an inventor and supporter of black entrepreneurship.

According to research by Tim Brady for the Coalition for the History of African American Contributions to the University of Minnesota, St. Paul at the turn of the century had a larger percentage of African Americans who owned their own homes than did any other city in the United States. In addition, the literacy rate among blacks was comparatively higher in Minnesota than it was in other regions of the country. "A thriving black press and a burgeoning number of African American community lodges, societies, leagues and protective associations encouraged and promoted educational advancement within the community," Brady wrote in "Young, Gifted, and Black: Ninety Years of Experience and Perceptions of African American Students at the University of Minnesota, 1882–1972."

It is important to note, however, that the number of blacks who owned businesses in Minnesota at this time was still very small. Some, like John Quincy Adams, occupied white-collar jobs before 1900. In addition to serving as the editor of the *Appeal* from 1887 to 1922, Adams was also appointed bailiff and acting clerk of the municipal court of St. Paul by Mayor Frank B. Doran in 1896. Other black professionals of this period included Bessie and Minnie Farr, who were probably St. Paul's first black schoolteachers; Dr. Valdo D. Turner, the city's first African American physician;

Frederick L. McGhee, its first African American attorney; and William F. "Billy" Williams, who was appointed as an executive aide in the governor's office in 1904 and remained in that post until 1957.

In March 1906, black attorney William T. Francis ran for the St. Paul assembly and received 9,080 votes, of which about 800 were cast by African Americans. He also actively campaigned against the Railroad Rate Bill, which, in the words of the *Appeal* on June 2, "if incorporated

William T. Francis, circa 1900. Minnesota Historical Society Collections

The Hallie Q. Brown boys basketball team, circa 1936. Minnesota Historical Society Collections

might make Jim Crow cars possible and probable all over the country as they are now in the God forsaken south." St. Paul congressman F. C. Stevens wrote directly to Francis and asserted his intention to fight the bill.

One of the anchors of St. Paul's African American community was established in 1914 with the Union Hall Association, which built a neighborhood center on one of its lots. This center became a gathering place for African Americans and community events, hosting activities in recreation, education, and the arts. In 1929, Union Hall became the Hallie Q. Brown settlement house.

Together with the Phyllis Wheatley House in Minneapolis, established in 1924, the Hallie Q. Brown settlement house provided a space where young African Americans could participate in competitive sports and athletics. The two settlement houses also sponsored adult sports and teams and hosted large tournaments that drew black athletes and teams from other states. The Brown and Wheatley houses became the center of the sports scene in the African American community. With the two houses located across the river from each other, a natural St. Paul–Minneapolis rivalry emerged between them.

Years later, in early 1941, the Hallie Q. Brown and Phyllis Wheatley houses would be joined by a third important organization serving the local African American community. Like Brown and Wheatley, the Ober Boys Club of St. Paul offered arts and recreation programs, as well as week-long summer camps, to help advance youth and families. The Ober Boys Club was operated by the Union Gospel Mission. For many decades, these three organizations were vital anchors in the community and, along with the black churches, were an integral part of African American life in the Twin Cities.

◆　◆　◆

Against the backdrop of the growth of black communities in the North during the early twentieth century, baseball, too, was on the rise. Spectators enjoyed the entertainment of watching the games, and for the players, the chance to show off their abilities was another method of building pride and self-esteem in the community. For those good enough to land on a team that was paying, baseball also became a way to earn a little extra income.

More African Americans were seeking to play baseball and to start teams in Minnesota. A column in the May 17, 1902, issue of the *Appeal* announced, "Amateurs Look for Many Games; Baseball Enthusiasm Strong Among Local Players. New teams are being organized and the old ones are kept busy answering challenges." At the professional and semipro level, some of the teams established during this era included the St. Paul Giants (founded 1905), the Colored Independent Club of Minneapolis (1907), St. Paul Colored Gophers (1907 and 1916), Minneapolis Keystones (1908), Hennepin Clothing Company of Minneapolis (1912), Minneapolis Colored Giants (1914), Colored Gophers (1914), Twin City Colored Giants (1915), Minneapolis Colored Gophers (1916), and the Duluth Steel Plant Colored Team (1917).

Minnesota's most notable black baseball team of this period was the original St. Paul Colored Gophers, founded in 1907. Any discussion of the

Colored Gophers must include the pioneer cofounder and manager, Phil "Daddy" Reid.

Born in Kentucky in 1854, Reid was an ambitious man who built an excellent reputation in St. Paul. In 1887 he was employed at the Eureka, which offered "Choicest Wine, Liquors & Cigars"; an ad lists Reid as one of the establishment's "entertainers." In February 1891, the *Appeal* announced the "grand success" of the grand opening of the new Eureka Saloon, relocated to 90 East Fifth Street. "The magnificent place," read the review, "was crowded from early in the evening until late at night with a jolly, good natured, liberal lot of the friends of the popular proprietor, Mr. J. H. Cunningham and manager, Mr. Phil E. Reid. . . . [A] large number of shekels jingled in the cash register during the evening."

By December 1898, Reid had his own business as "Importer of Fine Wines, Liquors and Cigars" (located at 373 Jackson Street in St. Paul) and was establishing himself as a successful entrepreneur and an influential member of the community. He participated in local politics, serving as president of the Fourth Ward Afro-American Democratic Club, and was involved with many lodges and societies. He was a fixture at galas and events for prominent African Americans in the Twin Cities. At a banquet honoring Joseph Gans in 1906, Reid was on a guest list that also included William T. Francis, John Q. Adams, Frederick McGhee, Valdo Turner, and other luminaries.

At some point, Reid turned his ambitions to baseball. He was determined to own the best black team around, and he quickly realized that dream. In early 1907, Reid and his business partner, John J. Hirschfield, formed what they called a "real colored baseball team": the St. Paul Gophers. They hired local star Walter Ball to recruit and organize a professional team, and he set off to bring in players who had a "national reputation"—at least within the world of black baseball. Ball and the owners wanted to make sure that the Colored Gophers roster was not limited to local amateurs but, rather, featured the top players they could get. As Todd Peterson notes in his *Early Black Baseball in Minnesota*, "Reid and Hirschfield focused their intentions on building the best ball club that money could buy."

The original Gophers squad was made up nearly entirely of players from Chicago, where Ball himself had been a member of the Union Giants. Many of these highly talented men had been playing with or against each other for years.

Play for Reid's Gophers began on May 4, 1907. The *Appeal* noted the arrival of the ball club in town earlier in the week, adding, "The St. Paul Gophers, Phil Reid's ball team, will make their first appearance on the St. Paul diamond at the downtown park this afternoon."

At the end of August the paper reported that the Gophers had played in "most of the principal cities of Minnesota, South Dakota, North Dakota, Iowa and Wisconsin. They have played 81 games, won 75 (22 being shut outs), lost 5, tied 1." The team also played to huge crowds, and, according to Peterson, the Gophers turned a profit and "traveled to places where no black team had gone before."

For an all-black baseball team in the early 1900s, traveling around Minnesota and the upper Midwest presented plenty of challenges. At the time, only about four thousand of Minnesota's nearly two million residents were African American, and more than 90 percent of them lived in Minneapolis or St. Paul. The Colored Gophers faced suspicion or even open hostility from residents and fans whenever they arrived in a new location, and the umpiring was often allied against them as well. "Most every place we play," Reid commented, "we have to stack up against ten men: the players and the umpire. And we rather expect it." Reports of inconsistent strike zones and outright bad calls were common.

Nevertheless, Reid and Hirschfield stepped up their recruitment in 1908. Walter Ball had left the Colored Gophers before the end of the previous season, but Irving Williams came on as manager and helped assemble a high-caliber team, again looking primarily to Chicago for new talent.

That year, Reid's Colored Gophers also saw a worthy contender emerge on the local scene—a rival based on the west side of the Mississippi River. Edward "Kidd" Mitchell, proprietor of the Keystone Hotel and Buffet on Washington Avenue in Minneapolis, was, like Reid, an ambitious entrepreneur and a prominent figure in the Twin Cities African American community. The Arkansas native was determined to take on Reid by build-

The 1908 St. Paul Colored Gophers. Minnesota Historical Society Collections

ing a baseball team that would be "faster and stronger than the Colored Gophers."

Mitchell's Minneapolis Keystones signed several top local players for the 1908 season, including hometown hero Bobby Marshall, who had suited up for the Colored Gophers in 1907. Acquiring Marshall not only meant benefiting from the talents of one of the city's most skilled players, it was also a shot across the bow, of sorts, to Reid and his Gophers. Three other former Gophers also played for the Keystones in 1908.

The two all-black professional teams would take on all comers, crisscrossing the Midwest for weeks at a time to play any team—white or black—willing to book them. Although the Gophers and the Keystones were among the toughest teams around, they were also big draws wherever they played, and other clubs gladly agreed to host them. In fact, booking one of these teams for a series could almost guarantee that the host team's season would be a financial success.

As the summer progressed, fans were calling for a playoff series between the Gophers and the Keystones. On July 19, the *Minneapolis Tribune* announced that the two teams had agreed to meet in a head-to-head series beginning in late August. After several scheduling attempts and some ducking on the part of Kidd Mitchell, the first of what would be five games was set for August 27.

Prior to their meeting, the Gophers had a record of 68–16–1 (.805) and the Keystones were 74–10–2 (.872). More than just a turf war, the series would grant the winning club bragging rights as the best black team in Minnesota and maybe the entire Midwest.

The Gophers won the first game 6–2 at St. Paul's Downtown Park. More than 1,800 fans were on hand to witness what Todd Peterson claims was the first-ever game in the Twin Cities between two black professional teams. "Considering the abilities of the combatants involved," Peterson adds, "it is not a stretch to say that it was the first game in Minnesota between two major league clubs."

The five games of the series were not played in succession but rather were spread out into late September. In between meetings, the teams continued with their regular schedules against other challengers.

The day after the Keystones game, the Colored Gophers were to play a team from Hibbing. Knowing his pitchers were hobbled with injuries, Reid called on his old pal Rube Foster in Chicago to fill in for the short-handed Gophers. Foster was perhaps the top pitcher in all of black baseball around the turn of the century, and he would later spearhead formation of the first organized black baseball league, the Negro National League, in 1920 (discussed in the following chapter). In 1908 Foster had helped the Leland Giants win the Chicago City League championship.

Foster arrived in St. Paul to face a strong Hibbing team made up of mostly ex–minor leaguers. With some 1,600 in attendance at Downtown Park, Foster led the Colored Gophers to a 5–0 victory, while not allowing any hits and walking just two batters.

A few days later, the Keystones and the Colored Gophers were back at it for their second meeting, this time playing in front of a huge crowd estimated at four thousand at Minnehaha Driving Park in Minneapolis. The game attracted visitors in town for the Minnesota State Fair as well as Black Elks conventioneers, and throngs of Gopher supporters made the trip from St. Paul. The Colored Gophers got on the scoreboard first, but the Keystones went on to triumph, 9–2.

With three weeks before the teams were to meet again, both resumed their travel schedules in Wisconsin and Iowa and around Minnesota.

At the next game of the series, the Gophers and the Keystones were offered a share of the gate receipts, with a cash prize going to the victor. Side bets further sweetened the pot for Reid and Mitchell. The Keystones won the third game 4–3 on Sunday, September 20, at Minnehaha Park. In an error-filled contest, the Minneapolis club broke a 3–3 tie in the bottom of the ninth to secure the walk-off victory. At Downtown Park the following day, the Gophers stayed alive with a much-needed 6–3 win in the fourth game.

With the series tied at two wins apiece, it all came down to the deciding fifth game, to be played at Nicollet Park, home of the American Association's Minneapolis Millers. The Gophers jumped on Keystone hurler Charles Jackson with four runs in the first inning, aided by several Minneapolis errors. Behind strong pitching from Dude Lytle, the Colored Gophers cruised to an easy 6–0 win, earning St. Paul the title of "colored champions of the Northwest."

Not content to rest on their laurels, "Daddy" Reid and his Colored Gophers stepped it up in 1909, with Reid embarking on an ambitious recruiting trip to the South that spring. He remained determined to have the best black baseball team in the Midwest—or at least west of Chicago—and the distinction seemed close at hand. On April 17, the *Appeal* reported that "Mr. Phil E. Reid, president of the Gopher Base Ball Club, is away down south in Dixie making up his team for this season. He has signed several good men and the line up will show a better aggregation of real ball players than last season. Manager Irving Williams is highly pleased with the outlook, and arrangements are being made for a series of games here that will tickle the cockles of the hearts of the fans of the Twin Cities."

Three weeks later the paper reported on Reid's return to the Twin Cities, "highly elated over his success." The May 8 edition of the *Appeal* listed the Gophers roster for the upcoming season: "Rat Johnson, catcher; Garrison, London, Williams and Taylor, pitchers; Binga, McDougall, Taylor and Wallace, infielders; Barton, Milliner and McCarry, outfielders. They open their third season today with a game at LaCrosse, Wisc."

Reid's club would win 88 games out of 116 in 1909, highlighted by Johnny "Steel Arm" Taylor's 28 wins. Johnny's brother Jim also played for the Gophers and carried a big bat. The Taylors had been wooed away from the Birmingham Giants. Dizzy Dismukes, a longtime pitcher and executive in the Negro Leagues, would rate Jim Taylor as the greatest black third baseman of all time.

Nicollet Park, Minneapolis

The 1909 St. Paul Colored Gophers. National Baseball Hall of Fame Library, Cooperstown, New York

The true test for Reid's Colored Gophers would come in a series against the Leland Giants of Chicago, which some contend ranks among the greatest black baseball teams ever assembled. It was announced in June that the Colored Gophers and the Leland Giants would play a five-game series in late July to determine "the world's championship" of black baseball. The series would be held at St. Paul's Downtown Park.

The *Western Appeal* of July 10 noted that "interest is at fever heat over the coming championship series between the St. Paul Gophers and the Leland Giants of Chicago." The paper further proclaimed that the Giants, "under the able management of the great Rube Foster, are unquestionably the greatest team of Afro-Americans ever organized." The local team, for its part, "is a most classy lot, being especially strong in the batting." The *Appeal* noted that several hundred supporters were expected to accompany the Leland Giants from Chicago, "while the Gophers will have the entire fandom of the Northwest to cheer them on."

The Leland Giants had been a powerful team over the previous years, besting the competition from all levels of play, both white and black. They had defeated the Minneapolis Millers four times in five games in September 1908. Featuring a formidable pitching staff that included former Gopher standout Walter Ball and the legendary Foster (who was sidelined with an injury before the series against St. Paul), the Leland Giants had won the Chicago City League in 1909 and would dominate the Chicago scene for many years to come.

Facing this imposing club from Chicago, the Colored Gophers won three of five games to claim the title as champions of black baseball.

In the opening contest, before a packed Downtown Park on July 26, the Gophers battled to an 8–7 lead before the Giants tied it up in the top of the ninth inning and then went ahead 9–8 in the eleventh. The hometown Gophers rallied in the bottom of the inning, however, to notch a 10–9 triumph. Bobby Marshall delivered the game-winning home run.

The Leland Giants rebounded with a convincing 8–1 win in the second game the following day, and in a matchup of the teams' ace hurlers, Chicago's Walter Ball led the Giants to victory over St. Paul's "Steel Arm" Taylor in game three.

In game four, the Gophers jumped out to a 4–0 lead after three innings but failed to get a runner on base after that. The Giants came back to close the gap before St. Paul secured a 4–3 win, tying the series 2–2.

In the deciding fifth game, "Steel Arm" Taylor got the start for St. Paul on just one day's rest, but it was his bat that made the difference. Taylor's two-run single in the bottom of the eighth against Ball put the Gophers ahead 3–1, and they held off the Giants in the ninth for a 3–2 final.

Blackball World Champion Series, 1909

Game 1: Gophers 10, Leland Giants 9, 11 innings
Game 2: Leland Giants 8, Gophers 1
Game 3: Leland Giants 5, Gophers 1
Game 4: Gophers 4, Leland Giants 3
Game 5: Gophers 3, Leland Giants 2

Despite Rube Foster's assertion, after the fact, that the games were merely exhibitions, the Gophers could lay claim to the title of champions of black baseball. They reinforced that position by defeating the Giants, 2–0, later that season in a game at Buxton, Iowa.

The St. Paul Colored Gophers and the Chicago Leland Giants were back at it in 1910. On July 23, the *Appeal* proclaimed, "What will unquestionably prove to be the most important event staged in semiprofessional base ball this season, to fans and lovers of the great national game, in and around the Twin Cities will be the series between the champion Colored Gophers of St. Paul and Frank Leland's famous Chicago Giants, for the world's championship." The five games would be played at St. Paul's Lexington Park from July 24 to 28.

The paper announced, "Special street car service will be furnished with preparations for handling one of the largest crowds ever assembled at Lexington Park on the opening day, Sunday, July 24." Train service from Chicago also brought many fans to see this highly prized series between two popular and talented teams.

"They came, they played, they conquered," said the *Appeal*, referring to the Giants, in the July 30 edition following the series. Although the Gophers took the opening game of the series, the Giants won the next four,

Lexington Park, St. Paul. Minnesota Historical Society Collections

thus allowing Chicago to reclaim the title of "champions of the world." The local fans were disappointed, but "lovers of base ball were highly entertained" by the fierce competition between the storied teams.

The Gophers were in existence under Phil Reid for four seasons (1907–10) and would win close to four hundred games, boasting a winning percentage of .807 that would be a source of pride for any major league team. The *Indianapolis Freeman* wrote in a 1910 preseason profile that the St. Paul nine had "established for themselves, their race, and city a reputation and record never before equaled." The *Freeman* also postulated that the Gophers were the most "sensational" team that the great Northwest had ever seen.

The St. Paul Colored Gophers set the standard for other African American baseball teams in Minnesota. Several teams even reused the Colored

Gophers moniker in the hope of capitalizing on the name recognition Reid had built and to help market their own teams as they barnstormed around the region.

A team using the Gophers name was in operation in 1911, managed by Bobby Marshall and owned and operated by Glover Shull. An article from the April 14 *Chicago Defender* made clear that there was no direct connection to Reid's team: "Manager Marshall wishes it distinctly understood that the 'Twin City Gophers,' are in no way connected with the famous Gophers of St. Paul, the club that was owned by 'Daddy' Reid. This is an altogether different aggregation."

In addition to unquestioned superior talents, the original St. Paul Colored Gophers maintained the lively cross-river rivalry with the Minneapolis Keystones. These two teams were among the best in baseball in the Midwest—regardless of skin color—and their records reflect their success.

The 1910 Minneapolis Keystones. Photo courtesy of Jason Miller

Walter Ball (seated on floor, far left) of the St. Cloud baseball club. Stearns History Museum, St. Cloud, Minnesota

A number of individual black ballplayers who took to the diamond in Minnesota during these opening decades of the twentieth century stand out for their accomplishments. Both Walter Ball and Bobby Marshall moved to the Twin Cities with their families when they were young boys before making headlines on the local scene as teenage athletes. Both would spend time in a Colored Gophers uniform as well. Billy Williams, born in St. Paul, was a multisport star in high school and had an opportunity to play baseball professionally but instead went to work for the governor of Minnesota.

Walter Ball

As discussed earlier, Walter Ball was a key figure in the formation of Phil Reid's mighty Colored Gophers team in 1907, but his career in baseball dates back to his teenage years in Minnesota.

Walter Ball of the Chicago Leland Giants, 1909. Chicago Historical Society, Chicago, Illinois

George "Walter" Ball was born in Detroit in 1877, and his family settled in St. Paul in the mid-1880s. According to James A. Riley's *Biographical Encyclopedia of the Negro Baseball Leagues*, Ball began his baseball career in 1893 with the Young Cyclones of St. Paul. He joined up with various other city teams until 1899, when he went to Grand Forks, North Dakota. He pitched for several North Dakota teams before returning to Minnesota to play for St. Cloud.

Ball's record as a pitcher for St. Cloud in 1902 was 17–7. He struck out 217 batters in 207 innings. As a hitter he wasn't too bad either, batting .307, with 18 doubles, five triples, and a home run. St. Cloud finished the year with a 29–12 record, and the team went on to win the championship of eastern Minnesota in 1902.

After considering several options, including staying in St. Cloud, in 1903 Ball was wooed by Frank Leland to play for the Chicago Union Giants. Prior to joining this team, Ball's experience had always been as the lone black representative on otherwise white teams; this was his first opportunity to play with an all-black baseball team.

In addition to Leland's Union Giants, over the next few seasons Ball spent time pitching for different teams in New York and Chicago, including the Cuban X-Giants, the Brooklyn Royal Giants, and the Quaker Giants of New York. (Obviously, "Giants" was a popular team name in black baseball at the time.)

In 1907, Ball returned to Minnesota to help Phil "Daddy" Reid and John Hirschfield organize and manage the St. Paul Colored Gophers. He also pitched for the club, but he left to rejoin the Union Giants before the end of St. Paul's season.

The following year, Ball jumped to the Minneapolis Keystones and pitched for the rivals from the west side of the river against the Gopher team he had helped build. Again, however, he would return to play for Leland to finish out the season in Chicago.

Ball continued to pitch into his forties. He spent two seasons with Leland's team, then known as the Chicago Giants, after it became part of the pioneering Negro National League formed in 1920.

Ball remained involved in baseball long after his playing days were over, as a coach and an organizer and in other roles. In recognition of his extensive and successful career in baseball, Ball was honored on the field in Chicago at the 1937 East-West All-Star Game, an annual Negro Leagues event. He was on the list of candidates for induction into the National Baseball Hall of Fame in 2006 but failed to make the first round of cuts by the Special Committee on the Negro Leagues.

Bobby Marshall

One of the greatest athletes in Minnesota history, Bobby Marshall was a multisport star in the opening decades of the twentieth century. Born in Milwaukee in 1880, Marshall moved to Minneapolis with his family

Bobby Marshall (standing, second from left) with the University of Minnesota Gophers baseball team

when he was a toddler. He participated in various sports at Minneapolis Central High School before going on to the University of Minnesota, where he competed in baseball, football, and track while also studying law. He was an all-conference end for powerful Gopher football teams from 1903 to 1906. But even a star athlete like Marshall was not immune to discrimination or personal slurs: he was described in the pages of the 1905 University of Minnesota *Gopher Annual* as a "lank-limbed child of sunny Ethiopia."

After graduating, Marshall tried his hand with several pro and semi-pro teams. He played semipro baseball in North Dakota, helped win a football championship with the Minneapolis Deans, and skated with the Struck Eagles hockey team. He even opened a law office in downtown Minneapolis.

On the diamond, Marshall played for both the Minneapolis Keystones and the St. Paul Colored Gophers. He was a key member of the 1909 Colored Gophers team that defeated the Chicago Leland Giants for the unofficial championship of black baseball. In 1912 Marshall helped form a team for the Hennepin Clothing Company in Minneapolis, and over the next two decades he put his talents and reputation to work for a number of different outfits, both locally and regionally.

Billy Williams

The career of Billy Williams illustrates, as well as anyone's, the dilemmas African Americans faced in the early 1900s. Despite being a stellar athlete and a standout player on several integrated baseball teams, Williams ultimately followed a path outside the sport, where the prospects were brighter than those on the baseball diamond.

Born in St. Paul in 1877, William Frank "Billy" Williams first gained notice as a multisport athlete at Mechanic Arts High School. A star in both baseball and basketball, he also set state high school records in track and field (specifically, the shot put) and played three years on the varsity football team.

Billy Williams of the Chaska White Diamonds

Billy Williams (middle row, second from left) with the Knoblauch Lands Carver team

His first experience in professional baseball was as a teenager with the St. Paul Spaldings, who, he remembered, "only asked of [him] long ball hits, and lots of them": race was never an issue. He continued to build his reputation as one of the best ballplayers around while with the top semi-pro team in St. Paul. He soon received offers from teams in Wisconsin, North and South Dakota, and Iowa. Other invitations came from as far away as New Jersey, New York, and Toronto.

In May 1902, Williams's name appeared in a newspaper item about baseball teams in the Twin Cities. "The Lennon baseball team, which has been in existence for several years," the article explained, "has been re-organized recently and is out after games with any amateur team in the state. It is composed exclusively of local talent and many of its members have enviable records on the diamond." Accompanying the article was a photo of Williams bearing the caption, "Captain of the Lennon team and the only colored player in that club." That a twenty-five-year-old African American would be named captain on an otherwise all-white team speaks to Williams's skills and the respect he garnered in the sport. He was listed in the lineup as the first baseman.

Two years later, on March 19, 1904, he was praised in the pages of the *Appeal* as "one of the most popular amateur baseball players in the state. He played last year with Chippewa Falls, Wis., the undisputed champions of Wisconsin. He is one of the members of the old Spauldings, which twelve years ago came into prominence by defeating the Litchfield, Minn., team then champions of the state. . . . It is a fitting recognition of his ability for 'Billy' Williams, the only Afro-American in the [St. Paul Amateur Baseball Association], to be chosen captain."

Williams was soon attracting attention from organized baseball. The Baltimore Orioles of the Eastern League asked Williams to join them, suggesting that he pass as an American Indian to avoid racist opposition. Orioles owner Edward "Ned" Hanlon wrote to Williams about playing for his team:

Mr. W. Williams
St. Paul, Minn

Dear Sir:
Your letter with the clippings which you will find enclosed were forwarded to me by Mr. Dooley from whom I have purchased the Montreal Baseball club. On receipt of this, send me your lowest terms to play in Baltimore.

Yours very truly,
Edward Hanlon
#1401 Mt. Royal Ave.
Baltimore, Md.

It wasn't an easy decision.

In St. Paul, which had a sparse black population, the only employment open to a young African American man was with the railroads or in hotels, where he was destined to work as a waiter, doorman, or shoeshine boy. Perhaps he could escape the trap by opening a small business of his own, but its success would depend heavily on the small black community and the generosity of a few whites.

These hard facts and more Billy knew. And these facts caused him to consider over and over in his mind the letter he had received from Hanlon.

In the end, despite his deep love for baseball, Williams declined the offer and instead accepted a job with Minnesota governor John A. Johnson, whom he had met in 1901. The newly elected governor had been so impressed with Williams that he offered him a job as an aide.

In a later interview, Williams reflected on the opportunity presented to him by Governor Johnson: "I happened to be a baseball player prior to my appointment as the governor's clerk, a position that is officially known as the governor's aide. Governor John A. Johnson, a personal friend of mine, offered me this position without any obligation on my part. He felt that there was very little future in baseball, and the position he was offering me meant, providing I made good, a more secure and successful life." Williams served as the assistant to fourteen Minnesota governors between 1904 and 1957.

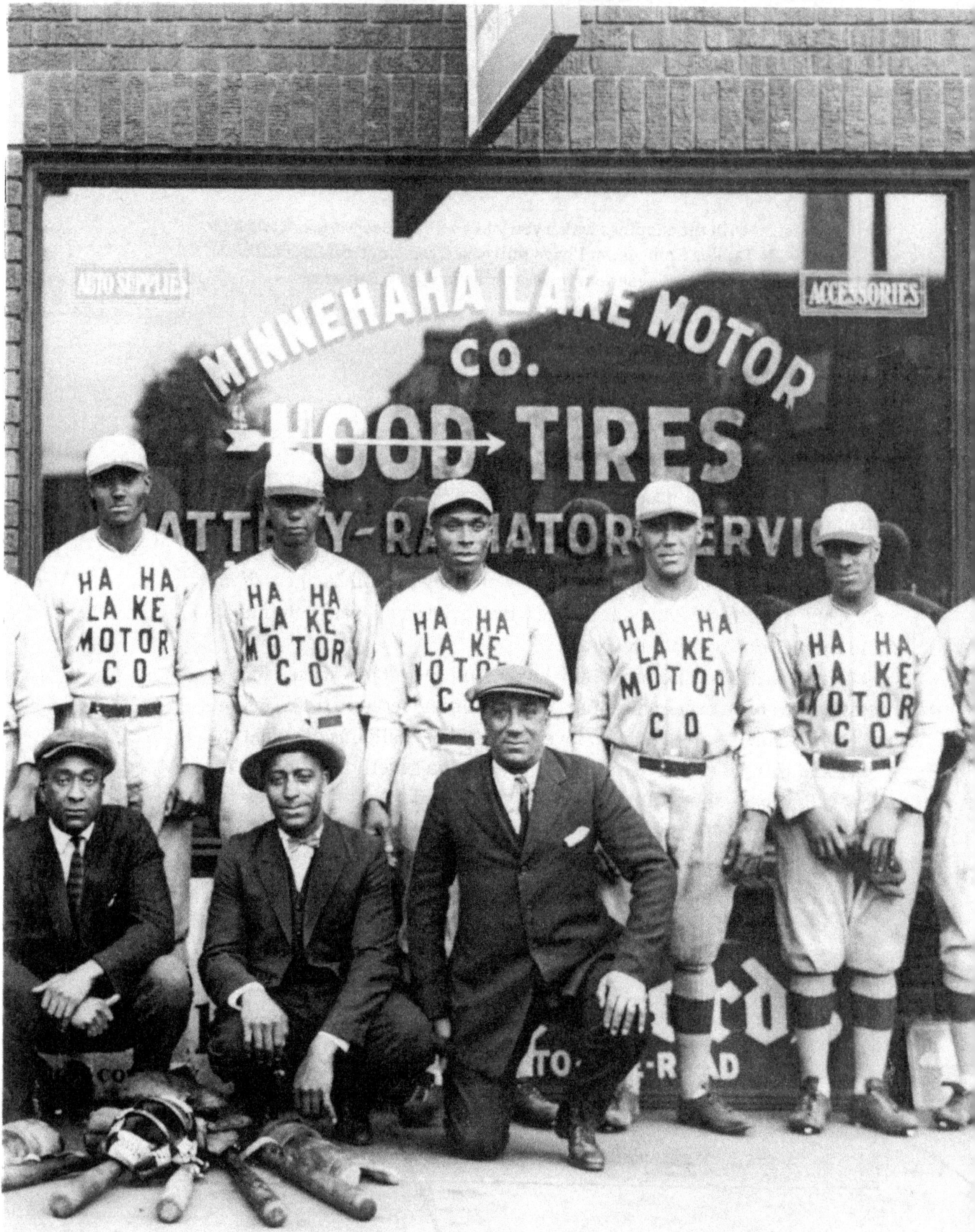
AUTO SUPPLIES
ACCESSORIES
MINNEHAHA
MOTOR
CO.
TIRES
HA HA LAKE MOTOR CO

·3·
The Roaring Twenties
Creating Their Own League

AT THE START OF THE 1920S, the United States was still recovering from World War I and the significant social changes that came with it. The Great Migration of African Americans from the South had been accelerated by the need for manpower in the defense industry in the North. This rush of black workers and residents also brought increased racial tensions to many northern cities, most notably during the race riots of the "Red Summer" of 1919.

In St. Paul, tensions were heightened when workers at the Armour packing plant, who were exclusively white, went on strike in 1919 and the company brought in African American laborers by the boxcar to work as strikebreakers. This ploy escalated racial anxiety in the city and led to greater hostility and discrimination against black residents, not only in employment but in housing and public accommodations as well. Even after many in the African American community had actively supported U.S. efforts during World War I, the number of economic and social avenues available to them continued to decline. Most working African American men could find employment only with the railroads as porters and waiters or other menial jobs in industries that did not provide a living wage.

African Americans were also moving out of the downtown area of St. Paul, following the black churches into the Rondo neighborhood. (Rondo was generally defined by Lexington Parkway on the west, Aurora Avenue on the north, Rice Street on the east, and Iglehart Avenue on the south.) St. Philips Episcopal Church, for example, was established at Aurora Avenue and Mackubin Street; the Pilgrim Baptist had moved from the corner of Twelfth and Cedar Streets downtown to its current location on Central Avenue; St. Peter Claver Catholic Church was on the corner of Farrington Street and Aurora Avenue. Once people moved into the Rondo neighborhood, the ability to move out of the area or be accepted in other parts of the city became increasingly constrained. In fact, socializing outside of the neighborhood was very rare, unless one worked elsewhere and was traveling back and forth between home and work.

The black-owned newspapers operating in the Twin Cities—there were several—were important forces in the community and kept the African Americans of Minneapolis and St. Paul well informed. Among them were the *National Advocate* and the *Minnesota Messenger* of Minneapolis and the *Northwestern Bulletin* and the *Appeal* of St. Paul; the latter two merged in 1924 to become the *Northwestern Bulletin-Appeal*. The papers reported on both local neighborhood news and national issues. In October 1923, the *Northwestern Bulletin* ran a front-page article noting a "Big Celebration for Rondo Street Opening." The St. Paul Negro Business League, the article stated, provided a plan for the opening of Rondo Street, "which will soon be paved" and is "rapidly becoming the bulk work of the race's commercial activities, and the paving from Western Ave. to Dale St. greatly augments the established program."

The newspapers also provided ample promotion for black-owned area businesses. The June 23, 1922, issue of the *National Advocate*, for example, included an item under the "Local News" column about "Askin & Marine Company, clothiers, located at 328 Nicollet Ave., Minneapolis." The paper referred to Askin & Marine as "the best people in our city to do business with," adding that the company has "in their employ the finest colored baseball team in the state, and the Company is proud of them."

Of course, it wasn't all uplifting stories being reported in the African American press. The pages of these papers were filled with tales of race riots spreading throughout the nation; of widespread lynching and the failure of the anti-lynching Dyer Bill in the U.S. Congress; and of the increasing discrimination and Jim Crow laws affecting the lives of African Americans in Minnesota, far north of the Mason-Dixon Line. As the *Appeal* reported on April 22, 1922:

The proposition to establish a playground for COLORED children in St. Paul is un-American and THE APPEAL is opposed to it.

One of the strange phases of Jim-Crowism in these days is the fact that nine-tenths of the plans to degrade the colored people into a pariah class are conceived in the brains of people who call themselves Christians. . . .

No greater evil could come to Saint Paul, to the white people as well as the colored people, than the attempt to segregate one group of citizens. It is the thing which will serve to inflame the fires of race prejudice. . . .

The decent self-respecting people of Saint Paul must fight the nefarious scheme to a finish. If you are a good American you should oppose it. IT MUST NOT BE!

Two weeks later, in its May 6 issue, the *Appeal* called out the Montgomery Ward Company, which "employs about 1,300 people at their magnificent plant on University Avenue," yet "only two colored men are employed and no colored women."

Just as race relations were entering another tumultuous period locally and nationally, the game of baseball was also undergoing many changes at the dawn of the new decade. In Major League Baseball, the controversy around the "Black Sox" scandal of 1919—in which Chicago White Sox players were caught taking bribes to lose the World Series—was a blight on the sport's image. But the emergence of the superstar slugger Babe Ruth and his towering home runs helped to reenergize the sport, and baseball was firmly established as the American pastime. Baseball's popularity was evident in the large number of pro and semipro leagues operating at the time, and town teams were the pride of many communities.

Black baseball was also on the rise, with new teams forming all around the country. African American ballplayers and team owners were becoming heroes in their neighborhoods. Rube Foster—the star pitcher of the Chicago American Giants and friend of St. Paul's own Phil "Daddy" Reid—saw that the growth of black communities in the North and the opportunities for jobs in the northern industries meant a larger and more affluent fan base. The time seemed right to launch an organized baseball league for black players and fans.

This was not the first attempt by black owners and managers to get together in an organized league. Following a banner year for black baseball

Phyllis Wheatley Settlement House

THE PHYLLIS WHEATLEY SETTLEMENT HOUSE opened its doors on October 17, 1924, and it soon became a centerpiece of the Twin Cities African American community. Originally established as a safe place for young black women to receive basic services, support, and guidance, it provided temporary housing, childcare, and health care and helped women develop professional skills. The Wheatley, as it was known, gradually expanded its focus and became the center of the black Minneapolis social scene, offering a range of recreational, educational, and arts programming. It was a frequent meeting place for civic and political activities. In addition, the Wheatley House was the only available lodging for visiting African Americans in Minneapolis during the age of Jim Crow, and many distinguished guests stayed there on their travels to the Twin Cities, including W. E. B. Dubois, Langston Hughes, Marian Anderson, and Paul Robeson. It also offered rooms to black ballplayers barnstorming through the Twin Cities.

The original building in North Minneapolis proved inadequate as the Wheatley House grew, and a second structure was built in 1929 on Aldrich Avenue North. It housed a child development center, gymnasium, auditorium, and apartments. The building was later demolished during construction of Interstate 94.

The Wheatley House also reveals another dimension of sports and the African American community, one that refutes the perception that team sports were not acceptable for female athletes and especially for black women and girls. A photo from 1925 shows a girls softball team hosted by the Wheatley House.

Another indication of women playing ball comes from a notice that appeared in the *Appeal* newspaper on June 29, 1907: "The Ladies' Ball Team of Minneapolis challenges any Ladies' Team of St. Paul to play one or a series of games, the first game to be played July 4th at the grand Barbecue, 49th St. and Washburn Ave. So. Address all communications to Mgr. Mrs. Emma Allen, 1915 4th Ave. So., Minneapolis, Minn." Apparently, the women of Minneapolis and St. Paul were also involved in the great intercity sports rivalry. ●

OPPOSITE: *Exterior view of the Phyllis Wheatley Settlement House located at 809 Aldrich Avenue North in Minneapolis.* Minnesota Historical Society Collections

ABOVE: *Baseball game at the Wheatley House, circa 1925.* Minnesota Historical Society Collections

BELOW: *Wheatley House girls softball team, circa 1925.* Minnesota Historical Society Collections

Andrew "Rube" Foster of the Chicago American Giants, circa 1920

in 1907, representatives from teams in Cleveland, Cincinnati, Detroit, Kansas City, St. Louis, Pittsburgh, Chicago, and Louisville looked to cash in on the momentum with a league, but scheduling conflicts and lack of financing doomed the undertaking before it could get off the ground. The St. Paul Colored Gophers, despite being among the elite teams of the day, were not included, since St. Paul was considered to be too far from the other cities.

The Twin Cities were again left out of the mix when, in February 1920, Rube Foster and the owners of seven other black baseball clubs from around the Midwest gathered at the Paseo YMCA in Kansas City, Missouri, to discuss establishing a league. The result was the Negro National League (NNL), which consisted of eight teams: Chicago American Giants, Chicago Giants, Cuban Stars, Dayton Marcos, Detroit Stars, Indianapolis ABCs, Kansas City Monarchs, and St. Louis Giants. Foster, owner of the Chicago American Giants club, was named league president. He would control every aspect of the league, including game schedules, team rosters, and equipment. He earned a percentage of all gate receipts as well.

Three years after the Negro National League formed, a rival organization, the Eastern Colored League (ECL), emerged. The ECL was established in 1923 with six clubs, all based on the East Coast: Atlantic City Bacharach Giants, Baltimore Black Sox, Brooklyn Royal Giants, Cuban Stars, Hilldale club from the Philadelphia area, and New York Lincoln Giants. Beginning in 1924, the champion teams from the ECL and the NNL would compete in the annual Colored World Series. The Kansas City Monarchs defeated Hilldale in nine games in the first series. Hilldale got its revenge with a win over the Monarchs the following year. Foster's Chicago American Giants topped the Bacharach Giants in the next and final two Colored World Series, in 1926 and '27. The ECL folded shortly after the start of the 1928 season.

Although neither Minneapolis nor St. Paul was among the cities included in the Midwest-based Negro National League, the new league did help to spur continuing interest in baseball among Minnesota's African Americans and in the local black press. The weekly *Minnesota Messenger* ran a regular "Baseball Notes" feature in its pages during the 1920s, covering the major leagues as well as Foster's budding organization. The *Northwestern Bulletin* commented on the popularity of the sport in its January 27, 1923, issue: "Baseball is one of the oldest and most favorite of all American sports, and there are some excellent players in our race."

Many of those "excellent players" from this era took the field for the Uptown Sanitary Shop, a dry cleaning business in St. Paul. The shop's baseball club was formally established in the spring of 1922 when, according to the *Northwestern Bulletin* of March 25,

> Enthusiastic baseball men met at the Uptown Sanitary System, 339 Wabasha Street, Wednesday night at 8:15, and organised the Uptown Sanitary Baseball Club. Mr. [Owen] Howell, proprietor of the Uptown Sanitary System, was elected president; Ralph Turner, vice president; Harry Davis, secretary. The president was given the power to appoint the manager. He then appointed John Davis, manager of the team of last year, to manage the team this year. The club will give a dance at Union Hall, the date to be announced later. The club organized with a membership of thirty. Those pledging their willingness to support the team were: Messrs. Lloyd Hogan, S. Montgomery, Roy Williams, Frank Ware, Harry Davis, W. Coleman, Dennis Ware, Samuel Stephens, G. L. Hoage, Otis Flood, James West, Otis Woodard, O. C. Cass, Harold Lewis, Lewis House, W. C. Willys, Leroy Hall, S. Whitlock, D. McGowan (Cherokee Bill), J. Brewer, Lionel West, Buster Clairborne, Gus Brown, John Davis and James Johnson.

The shop had been sponsoring a team prior to this formal announcement, however. The "Sports" column in the March 18 paper predicted that the "Uptown Sanitary Baseball Club is to be an A-1 team again this season. Five first class ball players have reported to the manager of this team, with the intention of securing a regular berth on this speedy set of 'diamond performers.' The proprietor, Mr. O. Howell, intends to make this club, the best ball team in the state."

Howell and Coach Dennis Ware continued to improve the team throughout the season. The *Bulletin* of May 13 noted that "the Uptowns have enrolled several new players, and with the abundance of material he has to work with, Coach Ware is rounding into shape a team capable of holding its own with any."

The 1923 Uptown Sanitary Shop baseball team, featuring Dennis Ware (third from left), George White (fifth from left), Bobby Marshall (sixth from right), and John L. Davis (fourth from right). Minnesota Historical Society Collections

Later that summer, on August 5, 1922, the *Bulletin* reported on the club's pioneering accomplishments: "The Uptown team is the only colored local team to play at [St. Paul's] Lexington Park. They have had at least one engagement at the park for the past three seasons. The Calgary Black Sox from Canada were the only visiting colored team to duplicate the Uptowns playing at Lexington."

Harry Davis's role as secretary for the team may explain the heavy coverage the Uptown Sanitary club received in the pages of the *Northwestern Bulletin*. He wrote a regular column in the paper called "Sport Notes," and he was a key figure in sharing information about local black athletes for many years. In addition, not only was Owen Howell the proprietor of the Uptown Sanitary Shop, he was also publisher of the *Bulletin*.

The March 25, 1922, edition of the paper announced Davis's hiring:

> In the appointment of Harry Davis as Sport Editor of the Bulletin, we feel assured one of the ablest athletes and sport followers of the Twin Cities has been secured to manage our sport section. He is a student at Hamline University and was a candidate for the basketball team there. He is a pitcher of great ability, having made his name famous on the "roster" of the Uptown Sanitary Baseball team of last year. He is also a member of the team this year. In addition to his ability on the diamond, he is one of the best basketball players in the Twin Cities having starred at forward position on the Sterling A. C. and Uptown Sanitary System quintets this season.

A graduate of the University of Minnesota, Harry Davis later became a minister for the Benton Avenue A. M. E. Church in Springfield, Missouri. The obituary for Harry's brother, John L. Davis, in April 1940 made note of Harry's athletic abilities, calling him "outstanding as an athlete when he lived in St. Paul" and noting that in his youth he was "well known as a baseball and basketball player." For his part, John served as manager and pitcher of the Uptown Sanitary team.

The Uptown Sanitary Shop team's main rival during this period was the Askin & Marine Company's Colored Red Sox, based in Minneapolis. The two would battle for bragging rights as the state's best during the 1920s, similar to the cross-river rivalry between the St. Paul Colored Gophers and the Minneapolis Keystones in earlier years. Established in 1922, the Askin & Marine Colored Red Sox were managed by Will Brooks and captained by local star athlete Bobby Marshall. The team reportedly went 30–9 during its first season of play.

The Askin & Marine team received ample coverage in the press as well. On May 6, 1922, the *Northwestern Bulletin* announced that "the Askins & Marines [*sic*] baseball nine has been greatly strengthened by several new additions to the team. Their team work has improved wonderfully, thus insuring the public of some real scientific baseball."

A front-page headline in the *Minnesota Messenger* on March 10, 1923, proclaimed, "Local Team All Ready for Coming Baseball Season," adding, "the Askin & Marine Clothing Co's Colored Red Sox have completed their team for the 1923 season and will have one of the fastest colored baseball organizations west of Chicago." ("Fast" was used to indicate skilled or talented in the parlance of the day.)

Piecing Together Player Identification

ONE OF THE CHALLENGES in researching black baseball players from a century ago is that information is sparse, and it is often difficult to identify players with certainty, especially individuals with similar names.

For example, John Barton Davis, a Kentucky native born in 1883, was recruited by Walter Ball from Chicago to play for the original St. Paul Colored Gophers in 1907. He spent a few seasons with the Gophers and then remained in the area for some time, playing for other teams. Then there's John L. Davis, who worked at the Uptown Sanitary Shop and was the team's pitcher and manager in the 1920s. It is not always clear which John Davis, both of them excellent pitchers, is being referenced in reports and photos from a century ago.

A photo of the 1923 Uptown Sanitary Shop baseball team illustrates the potential confusion (see page 51). In previous studies, the player featured in the back row, second from the right (and to the left of Bobby Marshall) was identified as John B. Davis, the pitcher previously with the Colored Gophers. However, Verlene Booker, niece of John L. Davis and sister of Hal "Babe" Price, saw this picture and said "that's Uncle John," adding that he worked at the Uptown Sanitary Shop in downtown St. Paul. Sylvester Davis, John L. Davis's son, later confirmed her identification.

The story of this Uptown Sanitary Shop team photo doesn't end there. While attending the funeral for Kenny Christian Sr.—an outstanding baseball and fast-pitch softball player, and one of the last known to play with my father—I met a woman named Wilma Neal. She mentioned that she had been trying to get in touch with me because she had an old baseball photograph from 1923 she wanted me to see. The photo was of the 1923 Uptown Sanitary Shop baseball team featuring Bobby Marshall and John L. Davis.

I told her I had seen the photo before, but upon closer examination of her copy, I noticed arrows pointing to two players. Wilma explained that her grandmother, Mama Duice Neal, put in the arrows to identify Dennis Ware and George White. After their successful playing careers were over, Ware was coach of the Collins & Garrick team in St. Paul, while White coached my father Louis and many others with the Twin City Colored Giants in the 1940s and '50s.

Wilma and her sister, Joyce Long, told me that their uncle, Roger Neal Sr., had been the executor of Ware's will and found the picture among Ware's belongings. Neal later donated the original photo to the Minnesota Historical Society. (In the "small world" department, I played pee wee baseball with Roger Neal Jr. in 1956, and we've been friends ever since.) I was later able to confirm the identification of Dennis Ware and George White with Norm "Speed" Rawlings and Gordy Kirk, longtime residents of St. Paul who knew both men. ●

Advertisement for the Uptown Sanitary Shop at 339 Wabasha Street in St. Paul

Askin & Marine Colored Red Sox, circa 1922

Both teams took their talents on the road to play teams elsewhere in Minnesota and the upper Midwest. In May of 1923, the *Northwestern Bulletin* told of the Uptowns' season-opening 15–3 victory before "an eight-day series up on the Range [beginning] the 27th of the month." The Colored Red Sox, meanwhile, "left in their new bus for Moorhead, Fargo and East Grand Forks, expect[ing] to be gone about a month." On June 23, the paper reported that the Red Sox returned from their "sizzling tour through the State," having gone 6–1 on the trip.

The two teams would finally go head-to-head in late September of 1923, a much-anticipated contest in the press: "The Uptown Sanitarys will cross bats with the Askin-Marine Red Sox of Minneapolis at Lexington

Park [on] Sunday, September 23 and Monday, the 24th at Nicollet Park in Minneapolis. . . . Great rivalry between these two clubs in the past three seasons has brought them together to settle argument of which is the best club." The day before the series was to begin, on September 22, the paper reported, "The Twin Cities baseball fans will be privileged to see two of the best games of the season Sunday and Monday. . . . The efforts of the captains of the two teams to get them together have at last been realized. Popular demand is responsible for the scheduled games."

The Uptown club earned the victory at Lexington Park, 6–4, while holding the Red Sox to three hits. St. Paul's "speed-ball ace" George Roach struck out fourteen batters in the game.

Even by 1925, the *Northwestern Bulletin-Appeal* was describing the Uptown Sanitary team as "composed of the best colored players in Minnesota." This traveling team was also, the article from May 30 noted, the only colored ball team in the state's Golden Valley League.

Uptown Sanitary and Askin & Marine were semiprofessional clubs. The players received some type of salary or, sometimes, a share of the net receipts from game admissions. Whatever the source, the compensation was rarely enough to pay the bills, and the players worked at other jobs as well. Because these teams were supported by local businesses, expenses were covered by the owners when game receipts were insufficient.

Another black team from this period that benefited from corporate sponsorship was the club fielded by the Chicago, Milwaukee & St. Paul Railroad. An article in the *Bulletin-Appeal* newspaper on February 24, 1924, stated that "this season a private car will be made available by the railroad company." The team, which "played 30 games last season and lost 12," was managed by Milton Williams of Minneapolis. The initial roster for the 1924 campaign, as reported in the paper, consisted of Maceo Breedlove, Bert Lewis, Dayton Blackburn, Fred Breedlove, Steve Banner, Richardson, Jess Reed, Joe Carter, Roy Lewis, Edgar Jackson, and Joe Scott. Maceo Breedlove would emerge as one of the state's top ballplayers in the following decade.

A number of other teams show up in accounts of local black baseball during the 1920s, some reappearing only sporadically, others maintaining a presence for several years. Harry Davis's "Sports" column in the May 6, 1922, edition of the *Northwestern Bulletin* revealed that "another colored baseball team has been organized in Minneapolis under the management of Alex Irvin. The Gray Devils, as they will be known here after, are young players who promise to make it hard for the other colored teams of that city to remain in the running. The new club has good financial backing, so all that the boys have to do is to produce the goods."

Other Minneapolis-based teams include the Minneapolis Browns, the Minneapolis Buffaloes, and the Potts Motor Company team. During their existence, these clubs and others would play teams from the Twin Cities as well as from all over Minnesota, the Dakotas, Wisconsin, and Canada.

While the number of black teams was on the rise, African Americans

The Minnehaha Lake Motor Company

A NEW TEAM HAS BEEN IDENTIFIED thanks to a photograph provided by Sylvester Davis, son of Johnny L. Davis. The photo is of the Minnehaha Lake Motor Company baseball team; the label at the bottom reads, "Johnny Davis's team." When Sylvester brought me the photo, I was able to identify Lee Davis (back row, third from the right) and Johnny Davis, the manager (in the front row, second from the left).

According to the *Minneapolis City Directory*, the Minnehaha Lake Motor Company was in business at 2920 Twenty-seventh Avenue South in Minneapolis (near the intersection of Minnehaha Avenue and Lake Street) from 1921 until 1935. It was owned and operated by Fred F. Rynda, and his brother Frank worked there as well during the first year.

As I tried to track down Fred Rynda, I came across two names: Francis Rynda and Florence Rynda, both in Montgomery, Minnesota. I called Francis, who said he didn't think his family was related to Fred, but he would ask his father. About ten minutes after we hung up, the phone rang and a gentleman on the other end said, "I understand you're looking for a relative of Fred Rynda. That was my uncle!" We talked for a while, and

he directed me to his brother Bob, who lived in the Twin Cities. When I connected with Bob a couple of days later, he said he was aware of the team but didn't know anything more about it.

A week later, I had lunch with Sylvester, his wife, and Bob Rynda to confirm the identity of the person we believed to be Fred Rynda, to Davis's right in the photo. In fact it was Fred, and Bob shared a number of stories about his uncle and his family in Montgomery. During a subsequent conversation, Bob talked about how Fred enjoyed sports and would bring his glove to play catch whenever he came to Montgomery for a visit.

I pointed out to Bob and Sylvester that a week earlier they hadn't known of their connection through this all-black baseball team from the 1920s, but now their families would be linked forever. I promised Bob Rynda copies of the photo to share with his family. He later found an original copy of the same team photo while digging further into his family records. ●

Minnehaha Lake Motor Company baseball team.
Photo courtesy of Sylvester Davis and Bob Rynda

were increasingly shut out from Minnesota's white leagues at the amateur, semipro, and professional levels. During the 1920s, the Association of Minnesota Amateur Baseball Leagues—the governing body of amateur leagues throughout Minnesota—issued a recommendation to all member leagues that they include in their bylaws a rule that "all colored players are barred." African Americans were thus eliminated from such amateur leagues as the Southern Minny, Western Minny, Southeastern Minnesota, Minnesota Valley, North Star, Wright County, Corn Belt, and North Central—in other words, from leagues all across the state. According to Armand Peterson and Tom Tomashek's *Town Ball: The Glory Days of Minnesota Amateur Baseball*, no black players appeared in Minnesota's prestigious state baseball tournament between 1927 and 1947.

The Southern Minny Baseball League, for one, had been in operation since 1912 and had teams located in more than thirty different communities at various times across southern Minnesota and northern Iowa. Among the member teams were the Mankato Merchants, Faribault Lakers, Winona Chiefs, Austin Packers, Owatonna Aces, and Fairmont Martins, to name a few. This vibrant and prestigious amateur league was completely off-limits to black players for more than two decades.

Still, black teams during this period were not limited to the heavily populated areas of the Twin Cities. The Pipestone Black Sox was an all-black team established in 1926 in the small southwestern Minnesota town. Research by Alan and David Muchlinski suggests that the team moved south of the border, to Marcus, Iowa, in late July of that year. In their 1997 article, "The Pipestone Black Sox," the Muchlinskis state that three other all-black teams were active in the region of southwestern Minnesota and northwestern Iowa, against whom the Black Sox played several games during the 1926 season. According to the Muchlinskis, the Pipestone Black Sox had a record of 8–3 against the three other all-black teams (the results of a twelfth scheduled game could not be located). The Black Sox, which boasted some former Negro League stars, reportedly had a 33–12 record against the white or integrated teams in Minnesota, Iowa, and South Dakota.

Regardless of location or racial makeup (white, black, or integrated), most baseball teams in Minnesota at this time were semiprofessional. Even players who were highly talented at the game they loved had to hold down other jobs to make a living. Many would work during the week and play baseball on weekends. If the team was going on the road, the players typically had to find somebody to cover for them at their jobs. Securing regular work was challenging enough for African Americans, and if baseball got in the way of getting the job done, players took a chance that business owners would not let them go.

Black ballplayers and others in the semipro ranks, however, were free from the "reserve clause" that ruled in organized baseball and which effectively locked players into one organization for their whole careers, or until the team decided to trade or release them. Those outside of major league baseball and its affiliated leagues were able to jump from team to team in search of the best contract or simply to land on a more talented roster.

As a result, players can be found on a number of different rosters over a short period of time. Bobby Marshall, for example, is referenced in box scores and newspaper accounts for at least seven different teams in the early twenties: Minneapolis Colored Gophers (1920), Askin & Marine Colored Red Sox (1922 and 1923), Minneapolis Colored Buffaloes (1922), Uptown Sanitary Shop (1923), Potts Motor Company (1925), St. Paul Colored Gophers (1925), and Minneapolis Colored White Sox (1926). He also went north to play with an all-white team in Estevan, Canada, along with pitcher Joe Davis, another homegrown talent.

In addition to jumping rosters for salary reasons or a new opportunity, players were sometimes "loaned" to other teams—usually with some sort of compensation to the original club—for a particularly important game or series, either to replace injured players or to improve that team's talent pool. Managers, owners, and players were constantly recruiting, talking with friends on other teams, doing whatever it took to get that key player to make the team stronger.

Besides Bobby Marshall, numerous black stars shone on the Minnesota baseball scene in the 1920s. Several elite hurlers from the Negro Leagues came to pitch for white teams in rural communities around the state, including Chet Brewer, Dave Brown, Webster McDonald, and John Donaldson—who, according to Todd Peterson, were "four of the greatest pitchers in blackball history." (Donaldson is discussed at length in the accompanying sidebar essay by Peter Gorton.)

Another Negro Leaguer who spent time in Minnesota was Leland C. "Lee" Davis. An outstanding catcher, Davis played for the Kansas City Monarchs and Chicago American Giants, and he would travel around the Midwest with Donaldson as a pitcher-catcher battery for barnstorming teams. Davis was not African American, however; he was a Ho-Chunk–Dakota Indian whose skin was too dark for organized baseball. When he wasn't touring with Donaldson or suiting up for Negro League teams, Davis bounced around with several teams in Minneapolis during the 1910s and '20s, including the Askin & Marine Colored Red Sox (as a teammate

John Donaldson

by Peter Gorton, founder of "The Donaldson Network"

> John Donaldson, best known colored baseball player in the world, is playing with the Bertha Minnesota team. For many years John was the star attraction of the All Nations. For quite a while he was the main cog in the Kansas City Monarch machine. He intends to stay in Minnesota quite a while. Donaldson is the only colored player on the Bertha team.
>
> *Northwestern Bulletin*, June 14, 1924

JOHN DONALDSON was the greatest left-handed pitcher of the pre–Negro League era. Prior to the establishment of the Negro National League in 1920, Donaldson had become a household name throughout the upper Midwest if not across the entire country. Donaldson's fastball combined with his devastating changeup and curve made opposing him in the batter's box a losing proposition. Today his legacy continues to be unraveled from the footnotes of history.

Donaldson first came to Minnesota as a member of the traveling minstrel troupe known as Brown's Tennessee Rats late in the 1911 season. W. A. Brown brought a sprawling tent show filled with vaudeville entertainment and a strong mix of traditional spiritual songs. The Rats entertained and barnstormed across northern Missouri, Iowa, and Nebraska and into Minnesota. The baseball act was where Donaldson's star shone most brightly. Donaldson led the Rats into Wells, Minnesota, for a season-ending contest against the loaded-up local ball club. Donaldson had already won over forty games that summer and was getting ready for some time off. The Rats traveled on the rails, bouncing from town to town and payday to payday. They came in on the morning train and followed the last whistle out in the evening. But Donaldson's skilled play took place outside of organized baseball. Segregation robbed him of the opportunity to showcase his talents on the larger stage; he was destined to make his living one diamond at a time.

Barnstorming was where Donaldson made his name as "The Greatest Colored Pitcher in the World." He would continue to frequent the diamonds of the Gopher State for the next decade. Starting in 1912, Donaldson signed with J. L. Wilkinson's World's All Nations team, based in Des Moines, Iowa. As the name implies, the club consisted of an advertised man of every nationality. Wilkinson's club brought racial diversity to each town it entered and proved that men of different races could live, eat, and play together. Nearly every summer the name *Donaldson* meant a huge number of spectators at the gates of local baseball fields. Fans in the Midwest wanted to watch major league talent. They read reports, heard firsthand accounts, and could see for themselves that Donaldson did not belong in their tiny one-horse towns. The color line brought him to their fields, and they enthusiastically shelled out their two bits to see this star player in exile perform.

Traveling black baseball teams were not new in Donaldson's time. The St. Paul Colored Gophers, Minneapolis Keystones, and dozens of other clubs had been playing in all corners of the state for years. Minnesota's brief summers saw some of the greatest ballplayers from the segregated era perform, and John Donaldson was poised and eager to add his name to the list of greats.

When the next attempt at organizing a Negro League occurred in 1920, John Donaldson signed with Wilkinson's Kansas City Monarchs and was called upon to pitch and play centerfield. After two seasons of unbalanced pay and even more unbalanced scheduling, Donaldson was asked by Wilkinson to revive the All Nations club as its manager and headline-grabbing draw. At that time Donaldson's "bankability" was well known, and for a season and a half he relived the barnstorming life that had built his reputation. But Donaldson soon soured on the constant travel in the new era of the automobile. When World War I limited passenger traffic on the nation's railroads and touring cars became more fashionable, barnstorming clubs began driving primitive automobiles from town to town. Auto travel proved to be increasingly difficult for Donaldson and his teammates. Faced with another season of life on the road, Donaldson changed course.

In the early spring of 1924, an organized group of entrepreneurs from the small community of Bertha, Minnesota, managed to entice Donaldson to headline the local semipro baseball team. Donaldson left the Kansas City Monarchs for a large pay increase, reduced travel demands, and the opportunity for continued stardom as the only black player on the Bertha Fishermen's all-white roster. With Donaldson on the mound, the Fishermen almost never lost. After three full seasons with Bertha (1924–25 and 1927), Donaldson compiled a record of 66–12 and dominated the semiprofessional ranks of the Gopher State.

According to Todd Peterson in *Early Black Baseball in Minnesota*, Donaldson "proved to be such a drawing card that the Bertha bleachers had to be expanded to house the overflow crowds who came to see him play." In 1926 Donaldson's services reached the lofty heights of $450 per month, making him one of the highest-paid black players in the history of the game.

In all, as one of the most traveled players black or white in the state's history, Donaldson played in or against more than 130 Minnesota cities. Before his long career ended in 1940, Donaldson had played with local nines in Alexandria, Bertha, Long Prairie, Madison, Minneota, Arlington, Cambridge, Lismore, Melrose, and St. Cloud. His legend remains in all of these cities today.

The latest pitching stats on Donaldson suggest that he belongs in the discussion of greatest black players in history. As of 2015, the Donaldson Network—a group of historians looking to rediscover the lost career of John Wesley Donaldson—has uncovered a verified career record of 398 wins and 157 losses with career strikeouts over 4,900. More than 150 of Donaldson's pitching appearances include no reported total for strikeouts, and thus his career numbers are vastly underrepresented. Donaldson's statistics include the highest known totals in wins and strikeouts of any segregated black pitcher in baseball

history. His career totals continue to rise as more information is being discovered daily.

Donaldson was included among the final thirty-nine Negro League candidates for induction into the National Baseball Hall of Fame in 2006, although he did not make the cut of the seventeen players and executives enshrined that year.

John Donaldson's legacies both as a man and as a ballplayer were forever changed by the bounds of the color line. As the folklore of Donaldson's prestigious career is reinvigorated, it is important to ensure that history does not rob Donaldson and other players like him of their combined legacies. The rightful place in history for these black stars is absolute.

John Donaldson. Photo courtesy of Peter Gorton

Lee Davis

of Marshall's in 1922), the Twin City Colored Giants, the Minneapolis Browns, the Minneapolis Buffaloes, and the Minnehaha Lake Motor Company. Lee's son, W. Harry Davis, would become a prominent boxing coach and administrator, a civil rights activist, and a Minneapolis civic leader; he even ran for mayor of Minneapolis in 1971. Harry Davis Jr., Lee's grandson, would be an all-conference baseball player at Minneapolis Central High School in the 1960s.

Bobby Marshall, Lee Davis, John Donaldson, George Roach, and countless others elevated the level of play on Minnesota's all-black teams and integrated town teams that toured the state. This burst of talent came just as the sport was experiencing a decade of significant growth throughout the country, including at the major league level. While information and documentation about these all-black teams is very difficult to come by, it is apparent from coverage in the local black press that Minnesota's African American communities were enthralled with following their local ballplayers and watching them succeed. This enthusiasm would continue into the 1930s, although new challenges brought about by the Great Depression and the continuing shadow of Jim Crow discrimination made it a tough row to hoe.

Black Baseball Rosters of the 1920s

In order to shed light on the various black baseball teams of this era, I have listed the team rosters as they appeared in the newspapers of the day. The information provided is not always complete or consistent, and the names and positions are given as they were originally printed. For some, only the manager, pitcher, and catcher were listed. Some players show up on more than one team's roster within a given year as well as from year to year.

For the 1920s, to supplement the rosters that were listed in the newspapers, I was fortunate to have access to the original scorebook of Paul Gerhardt of the Oxboro Heath team of Bloomington, through a chance meeting with his son, Lyle Gerhardt. The book included score sheets for six games between Oxford Heath and the Uptown Sanitary Shop of St. Paul and one with the Potts Motor Company team of Minneapolis. All references to score sheets in the following list are courtesy of Lyle Gerhardt.

1921 UPTOWN SANITARY SHOP
From score sheet of September 18
(listed by batting order)

Coleman (SS)
Dennis Ware (3B)
J. West (OF)
L. West (1B)
Schuck (OF)
Perry (2B)
Gizter (OF)
Davis (P)
Flood (C)
Harris (utility)

1922 MINNEAPOLIS BUFFALOES
From March 23, April 29, and May 6
editions of Northwestern Bulletin

James L. Bacon (manager)
Joe Davis (P)
Lee Davis (C)

Oxboro Heath Scorebooks

IN JULY 2011, I was giving a presentation about black baseball at the library in Burnsville, Minnesota. Right before my talk, Lyle Gerhardt showed me a scorebook of games from the 1920s. He pointed to the name "White" on one of the pages and asked if it was my father. Since that particular game had taken place on May 29, 1927, and my father wasn't born until February 29, 1928, I could safely say that it was a different White playing centerfield that day.

A short time later, I visited Lyle and his wife, Juanita, at their home in Burnsville and reviewed the scorebook, which recorded games involving Oxboro Heath, a white team from Bloomington for which Lyle's father, Paul Gerhardt, had played. The book contained score sheets of seven games in which Oxboro Heath played all-black teams from either St. Paul or Minneapolis. I was honored when Lyle agreed to let me make copies from the book—a true artifact of Minnesota baseball history and, with its hard broadcloth cover and crumbling yellowed pages, a real treasure.

Paul Gerhardt had been the manager and a player for Oxboro Heath, and he also owned the farmland on which Metropolitan Stadium would be built for the Triple-A Minneapolis Millers, later serving as the home of the Minnesota Twins from 1961 to 1981. (Today, this site is taken up by the Mall of America and IKEA.) According to Lyle, after the land was sold, Paul was hired by the Millers to be the stadium's assistant groundskeeper.

In my research I was able to find four articles related to the games played in Bloomington: Potts Motor Company vs. Oxboro Heath, May 24, 1925, and Uptown Sanitary Shop (St. Paul Colored All Stars) vs. Oxboro Heath, May, 29, 1927. I've found some discrepancies with spellings of names, depending on who was managing the scorebook. Really, it's no surprise: the same could happen today.

In subsequent research, I came upon an advance article on the May 29, 1927, game between Oxboro Heath and the Uptown Sanitary Shop team (then playing as the St. Paul Colored All Stars), for which Gerhardt had a score sheet. The article, from the *St. Paul Echo*, stated that the game would be played at Callan Meadows, a location with which I was unfamiliar. Lyle explained that it was just across the old Cedar Bridge over the Minnesota River. I found a plat map indicating land owned by James Callan bordering the river, and I learned from talking to several individuals that the ball field was next to a bar and boat landing. It was quite a distance from St. Paul and Minneapolis back in those days, with no easy method of transportation for a black baseball team. Lyle also shared that some of his friends played softball on this field in the 1960s. Today the land is part of the Minnesota Valley National Wildlife Refuge. ●

OPPOSITE: *Baseball team at Oxboro Heath, Bloomington, 1921.* Minnesota Historical Society Collections

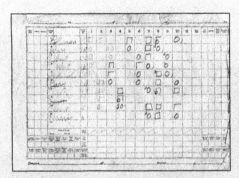

Score sheet for Uptown Sanitary Shop team vs. Oxboro Heath, September 18, 1921. Courtesy of Lyle Gerhardt

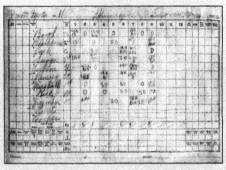

Score sheet for Potts Motor Company team vs. Oxboro Heath, May 24, 1925. Courtesy of Lyle Gerhardt

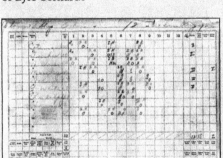

Score sheet for Uptown Sanitary Shop team vs. Oxboro Heath, August 27, 1922. Courtesy of Lyle Gerhardt

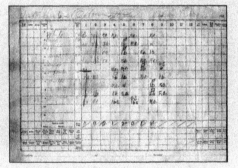

Score sheet for Uptown Sanitary Shop team vs. Oxboro Heath, August 8, 1926. Courtesy of Lyle Gerhardt

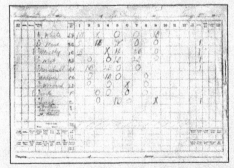

Score sheet for Uptown Sanitary Shop team vs. Oxboro Heath, August 5, 1923. Courtesy of Lyle Gerhardt

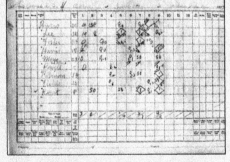

Score sheet for St. Paul Colored All Stars vs. Oxboro Heath, June 12, 1927. Courtesy of Lyle Gerhardt

1922 UPTOWN SANITARY SHOP

From score sheet of August 27 (listed by batting order); additional names from May 13 edition of Northwestern Bulletin *indicated with an asterisk*

---

*Owen Howell (owner)

John Davis (*manager/P)

Coleman (3B)

Tucker (2B)

Dennis Ware (SS)

Moseley (1B)

DuLov Hogan (CF)

George White (LF)

Rudolph (RF)

Howard (C)

Roach (P)

Harry Davis

*Frank Ware

*J. West

*Burton (P)

1922 ASKIN & MARINE COLORED RED SOX

From September 30 edition of Minnesota Messenger

Ike Bradley (1B)

Will Brooks (captain/utility)

Speed Coleman (2B)

Joe Davis (P)

Harry Davis (2B)

Lee Davis (C)

E. Jackson (RF)

Harold Lewis (SS)

Harry Lewis (LF)

Bob Ramsey (CF)

1923 MINNEAPOLIS BROWNS

From February 24 edition of Minnesota Messenger

Chas. L. Gooch (president)

W. A. Smith (manager)

Eddie Blackman

Isaac Bradley

John Craig

Joe Davis

Lee Davis

Art Jones

Harold Lewis

Otto Mitchell

Bob Ramsey

Jesse Reed

Gilbert Rice

M. Richards

Joe Williams

Lefty Williams

**1923 ASKIN & MARINE
COLORED RED SOX**

From March 10 edition of Minnesota Messenger; *additional names from team photo in June 16 edition of* Northwestern Bulletin *indicated with an asterisk*

Will (Bill) Brooks (utility)

B. Coleman (3B)

Joe Davis (P)

Lee Davis (C)

George C. Howard (LF)

Edgar Jackson (RF)

Roy Jackson (CF)

Harold Lewis (1B)

Harry Lewis (RF)

Coot Longley (SS)

Bob Marshall (2B)

Sonny Lucas (utility)

Lefty Wilson (P)

Tommy Young

*Eddie Blackman

*George Coleman

*Bert Jones

*Bert Tucker

*W. R. McKinnon (promoter and financial backer)

1923 UPTOWN SANITARY SHOP

From score sheet of August 5 (listed by batting order); additional names from May 12 edition of Northwestern Bulletin *indicated with an asterisk*

George White (LF)

Dennis Ware (3B)

Mosley (1B)

J. West (RF)

Bobby Marshall (SS)

Walker (CF)

O. Woodard (2B)

Roach (P)

Luck (C)

Foster

Lee Davis

Harry Davis

*Johnny Davis (P)

*Hogan

*Howard

*Stephens

*Lawrence Tucker

1924 CHICAGO, MILWAUKEE & ST. PAUL RAILROAD (C.M. ST.P)

From February 24 edition of Northwestern Bulletin

Milton Williams (manager)
Steve Banner
Dayton Blackburn
Fred Breedlove
Maceo Breedlove
Joe Carter
Edgar Jackson
Bert Lewis
Roy Lewis
Jess Reed
Richardson
Joe Scott

1925 UPTOWN SANITARY SHOP

From January 31 edition of Northwestern Bulletin

Owen Howell (owner)
John Davis (manager/P)
Dennis Ware (assistant coach)
Savannah Fields (SS)
Loyd Hoggatt
Timothy Howard (C)
Eugene Jackson (LF)
Harold Roach (P)
Lawrence Tucker (3B)
James West (LF)
Lionel West (1B)
George White (LF)
Johnnie Williams (utility)
Otis Woodard (CF)

1925 POTTS MOTOR COMPANY

From score sheet of May 24 (listed by batting order); additional names from May 23 edition of Northwestern Bulletin *indicated with an asterisk*

*Bill Brooks (manager)
Eddie Boyd (SS)
Blackborne (2B)
Luck (C)
B. Suggs (3B)
E. Jackson (LF)
Ramsey (CF)
Bobby Marshall (1B)
H. Rice (RF)
Bill Freeman (P)
Roberts (P)
Cooper (C)
*D. Blackman (OF)
*A. Freeman (OF)

1926 UPTOWN SANITARY SHOP

From score sheet of August 8 (listed by batting order)

White (LF)
Roach (RF)
Lee (CF)
Hunt (3B)
Brown (P)
Parker (1B)
Fields (SS)
Powers (2B)
Winnie (C)

1927 UPTOWN SANITARY SHOP
From score sheet of May 29
(listed by batting order)

DuLove (CF)
Lee (3B)
Mays (1B)
Roach (P)
White (LF)
Winnie (C)
Robinson (2B)
Fields (SS)
Foster (RF)
Powell (utility)

**1927 ST. PAUL COLORED ALL STARS
(FORMERLY UPTOWN SANITARY SHOP)**
From score sheet of June 12
(listed by batting order)

Powers (2B)
Lee (3B)
Foster (RF)
Harris (1B)
Mays (CF)
Powell (C)
Robinson (LF)
Fields (SS)
Hunt (P)

Score sheet for Uptown Sanitary Shop team vs. Oxboro Heath, May 29, 1927. Courtesy of Lyle Gerhardt

·4·
The 1930s
Promises, Challenges, and the Great Depression

THE STOCK MARKET CRASH OF OCTOBER 1929 sent the world into a global economic depression that would continue throughout the 1930s. Millions of Americans lost their jobs or homes or life savings—or all of the above—and African Americans were hit particularly hard. With employment opportunities extremely scarce, blacks were the last hired and first fired. They were even denied many of the lower-paying and menial jobs to which African Americans had been restricted previously, such as hotel bellhops and waiters. They had to fight desperately to hold on to the few positions made available to black workers.

Jim Crow also continued to rear its ugly head. Although Minnesota law did not allow for the segregation of public transportation, housing, or schools, segregation was a part of everyday life. The University of Minnesota maintained discriminatory practices in housing and other aspects of campus life. Many local restaurants flatly denied service to black customers. Touring black entertainers and athletes were not welcome in area hotels and had to stay with local residents or in one of the few available settlement homes. Restrictions on freedom were felt deeply by African Americans throughout the state.

On February 21, 1936, the *Minneapolis Spokesman* reported on a statement released by the National Negro Congress (NNC) condemning "the vital problems of Civil Liberties, including lynching, Jim-crowism, residential segregation, disfranchisement, gag-laws, destruction of freedom of speech, press and assembly, and the increasing Fascist threats to the rights of the Negro and other minority groups." The resolution by the NNC to fight for the rights and civil liberties guaranteed by the U.S. Constitution was fully supported by the *Spokesman*, as these concerns were as great for African Americans in Minnesota as they were elsewhere. (Founded in 1934, the *Minneapolis Spokesman* continues to publish a newspaper, now under the name *Minnesota Spokesman-Recorder*, and is the oldest African American–owned business in Minnesota.)

◆ ◆ ◆

The Great Depression of the 1930s had a tremendous impact on black baseball as well. Not only did African American communities suffer greatly with the lack of available jobs and other hardships, it was particularly difficult for their ball clubs to stay afloat. Indeed, the overall number of baseball teams, both white and black, declined during the decade. Barnstorming teams struggled to scrounge up the necessary cash to cover gas and other travel expenses. And even if they were able to get to their destination, there was little guarantee that enough spectators would show up to make it worth the trip.

The Association of Minnesota Amateur Baseball Leagues continued its ban on black players, initiated in 1927. The Negro National League still had no team based in the Twin Cities, and the Negro American League debuted in 1937 with teams from the Midwest and South, but none in Minnesota. Organized baseball—the major league and all its affiliated minor leagues—also maintained its firm policy of segregation.

But despite these numerous barriers, many of Minnesota's African American ballplayers were able to find opportunities to play and thrive on the diamond during this challenging time. Among the all-black teams in Minnesota that appear in accounts from this period were the Colored House of David, St. Paul Colored Gophers, John Donaldson All-Stars, St. Paul Monarchs, Minneapolis Colored Giants, Minneapolis Keystone Tigers, Phyllis Wheatley House Cardinals, Collins-Garrick, and the Twin Cities/Twin City/St. Paul Colored Giants. (Team names would sometimes appear with slight variations in the papers, particularly in reference to the club's home designation.)

The Wheatley Cardinals are mentioned in a 1937 article as playing in the Minnesota Valley League. Although the state's governing body of amateur baseball still rejected black players and teams, it appears that black teams were occasionally allowed to participate in league play during the regular season, but not in postseason tournaments. Pitcher Don Strawder, Bert Lowry, Clemons Rooney, and Bubba Brown are among those who played for the Wheatley team that year.

A piece in the July 23, 1932, edition of the *Twin City Herald* discussed the St. Paul Monarchs, "organized two years ago by Frank Boyce." The Monarchs had been playing out-of-town engagements almost exclusively since their formation in 1930, but, according to the *Herald*, "Mr. Boyce has decided to bring the boys before the home fans, hence the game at Lexington Park against the St. Paul Milk team has been arranged. It will be the first time a colored team has appeared at the St. Paul ball park for a long time."

The article lists among the Monarch players first baseman Bobby Marshall. More than two decades after he played with the St. Paul Colored Gophers during the championship season of 1909, the "grand old man" was in his fifties. Marshall was just one of several famed players of the 1920s who were still at it, fulfilling their passion for the game while attempting to earn a few dollars barnstorming around the state and beyond. Others were only just making their presence known to black baseball fans. A few of the prominent names of the 1930s were Maceo Breedlove (outfielder), Lee Davis (catcher), Jake "Rocking Chair" Foots (catcher), Bill Freeman (pitcher), Reggie Hopwood (outfielder), Jimmy Lee (second baseman), Victor McGowan (outfielder), George Earl Roach (pitcher), Dennis Ware (catcher), George White (outfielder), and Chinx Worley (outfielder).

The Colored Giants, under the supervision of Jake Foots, started practice in early May 1935 for their first game, at Lexington Park, against the white House of David traveling team. In August of that year, the Keystone Tigers played the Twin City All-Stars, a traveling white team led by former major leaguer Bubbles Hargrave. The Tigers were the first black team to play at Nicollet Park in seven years.

With the fluid nature of teams during this period, and as players sought out the best payday, some top ballplayers left the Negro Leagues for other ventures. One of the most notable examples was the semipro team owned by businessman Neil Churchill of Bismarck, North Dakota. Churchill began recruiting black players to the formerly all-white team shortly after he became owner. Among the Negro League players to join the Bismarck club were Quincy Troupe (centerfielder/catcher), Red Haley (infielder/outfielder), Ted "Double Duty" Radcliffe (pitcher/catcher), Satchel Paige (pitcher), Chet Brewer (pitcher), Hilton Smith (pitcher), and Barney Morris (pitcher).

This team was put together to win the inaugural National Baseball Congress (NBC) championship tournament in Wichita, Kansas, a competition involving semipro and amateur leagues from around the country. The Bismarck team had an outstanding season in 1935 and went on to win the tournament, but was never allowed to play again in that competition.

1935 Bismarck baseball team

Satchel Paige was particularly impressive in the series, winning four games and striking out 66 batters in 39 innings. Following the tournament, *Minneapolis Tribune* sports columnist George Barton noted the potential value of a pitcher like Paige: "Bismarck has in Satchel Paige, Negro, a pitcher, who, if he was white and eligible to play in organized baseball, would bring around $100,000 in the open market. He possesses everything a great pitcher must have." Many major league scouts attended the tournament, but they were there to observe the white talent. While more than a dozen players at the NBC were signed by major league organizations, the best player of the whole tournament—Paige—was never even considered.

As a pretournament warm-up, Churchill's Bismarck team, with its high-priced hired guns, had hosted a semipro squad from Minnesota for a three-game series. According to Tom Dunkel in his book *Color Blind: The Forgotten Team that Broke Baseball's Color Line*, Bismarck was coming off a streak of nineteen wins in their previous twenty games. The Twin City Colored Giants, meanwhile, were a "second tier traveling club" whose players worked nine-to-five jobs and played mostly on the weekends. Churchill, as Dunkel puts it, "wanted a weak opponent to push around on the eve of the Wichita tournament."

True to expectations, Bismarck won the three games handily—including a 21–6 thrashing in the finale with Paige on the mound. But the Colored Giants did show off their top-notch outfielder, Maceo Breedlove, who proved that he could play with the best of them.

Breedlove, who had already collected a home run and two doubles off Paige in the final game, came up in the ninth inning with two outs and a runner on first base—and Bismarck holding a seventeen-run lead. After fouling off a few fastballs, Breedlove sent Paige's next offering, a curveball, deep into leftfield for a two-run homer. (It should be noted that the ever-confident Paige had employed one of his classic ploys and told his fielders, other than the catcher and first baseman, to leave the field while he disposed of the opposing batters. Other than the single and Breedlove's drive, Paige struck out the side in the ninth.)

Although Paige's feats (and shenanigans) were the big story of the series, Breedlove's stats in the three games against this integrated all-star team highlight why he is considered one the greatest hitters in the history of Minnesota black baseball. In the series, Breedlove went 8 for 13, including two doubles and three home runs, for a .615 batting average and 1.462 slugging percentage. Other than his two shots against Paige, Breedlove also homered against Hilton Smith in the second game of the series; Smith, a Hall of Famer like Paige, is considered one of the greatest pitchers in Negro Leagues history.

Originally from Alabama, Breedlove arrived in Minnesota in 1922 and played with various barnstorming teams until he retired in 1944. In later years, he worked as a beer vendor for Twins games at Metropolitan Stadium. He died in 1993 at the age of ninety-two.

During a visit to Minnesota in 2003, former Kansas City Monarch and Negro Leagues legend Buck O'Neil called Breedlove a great hitter, noting that he "could have played with any of our [Monarchs] teams." In a *Star Tribune* piece upon Breedlove's death, Harry Davis, son of Twin Cities baseball legend Lee Davis, said that Breedlove was "as good as [Kirby] Puckett and [Dave] Winfield."

The centerfielder on the Colored Giants squad that faced Churchill's loaded Bismarck team was Reginald "Hoppy" Hopwood, a St. Paul native. Hopwood had also played outfield briefly for the Kansas City Monarchs in 1928. He was known for his speed on the base paths, according to his daughter, Victoria Hopwood. Reggie or Rudy, as he was also known, would amend his birth certificate at least three times—from February 5, 1900, to 1903 and finally to 1906. It was not uncommon for players to adjust their actual ages to make them younger in the hopes of getting a shot with a team. (Satchel Paige was one of the most famous employers of this strategy.)

Victoria Hopwood recounted how her father told her stories of the rough existence for barnstorming black teams in those days. Hopwood noted that when they beat an all-white team, sometimes they had to pack up and leave town immediately after the game, occasionally dodging a volley of rocks being thrown at them by supporters of the local team. And like most black players of the time, Hoppy and his teammates, restricted from enjoying the comforts of hotel rooms, had to find accommodations in private homes when on the road.

Hopwood later worked on the railroads, and his daughter recalls how he loved going to Minnesota Twins games whenever he was back in town. Victoria remembers a "sadness in his eyes" because, she believed, he longed to be on the field playing major league baseball.

By 1937, both Hopwood and Breedlove had moved on from the Colored Giants, but the team had acquired another phenomenal—if nontraditional—star for its roster: a sixteen-year-old pitcher named Marcenia Lyle "Toni" Stone. As much as her youth was a novelty, what really set her apart was her gender: she was the only female player in baseball at the time.

Stone pitched several games for the Colored Giants in 1937. "She was as good as most of the men," remembered teammate Harry Davis. Jimmy Lee, in his "In the Sport Light" column for the *Minnesota Spokesman-Recorder*, wrote on July 30, 1937, that the Colored Giants have "the distinction of having a girl pitcher on its roster. No other team in the Northwest can boast the same." Lee, who also played second base for the Twin City Colored Giants, continued, "Miss Marcenia Stone, 16-year-old girl athlete, has been doing much to amuse the fans with her great catching and wonder power hitting. Miss Stone is truly a typical athlete and we do not hesitate to predict that she someday will acquire the fame of one 'Babe' Didrickson," the track, basketball, and golf star.

Stone, now seventeen years old, was back with the Colored Giants in 1938. One of the

Reginald "Hoppy" Hopwood of the Kansas City Monarchs, April 1928. Courtesy of the Hopwood family

highlights of that season was on Labor Day, September 5, when the Giants took on a team from Connorsville, Wisconsin, that featured a future major league player, Andy Pafko. Stone didn't start the game but came in to play leftfield in the eighth and, according to the account in the *Dunn County News* on September 7, "made two difficult catches in the outfield."

"Tom Boy" Stone, as she was sometimes referred to in the press, went on to have an illustrious career in baseball. She joined up with the semipro San Francisco Sea Lions after World War II and played for the New Orleans Creoles beginning in 1949. She became the first woman in the organized Negro Leagues when she signed with the Indianapolis Clowns in 1953 to play second base. Stone retired from the pro ranks after the '54 season (the same year, coincidentally, that the All-American Girls' Professional Baseball League—which had banned Stone because of her skin color—played its final season).

Stone died on November 2, 1996, at the age of seventy-five. The following year, St. Paul's Dunning Field—where she had played early in her career with the Colored Giants and others—was renamed Toni Stone Field by the city of St. Paul. Despite the official dedication ceremony, the field continued to be

Box score of game between Twin City Colored Giants, featuring Toni Stone, and the team from Connorsville, Wisconsin, September 5, 1938

GIANTS DEFEATED BY CONNORSVILLE

Darby Worman Pitches Effective Ball for the Winners.

Connorsville—Connorsville won, 13-4, from the Colored Giants in a Labor day game here. Darby Worman pitched a fine game for the winners, allowing but five hits.

The Colored team started a 16-year-old pitcher who Connorsville nicked for four hits and five runs in the first inning. Roach then replaced Richardson in the first inning.

In the eighth the Giants put in "Tom Boy" Stone, a girl, who played left field. She made two difficult catches in the outfield.

The Boxscore

Giants	AB	R	H	E
Worley, ss	5	1	2	1
Vickes, 2b	4	1	1	0
White, lf	2	0	0	2
Davis, 3b	4	0	0	1
Jackson, T., cf	4	1	1	0
Ford, 1b	4	0	0	0
Guyden, rf	3	1	1	0
Jackson, E., c	3	1	1	0
Richardson, p	0	0	0	0
Roach, p	4	0	1	0
Tom Boy Stone, lf	1	0	0	0
Totals	35	4	5	4

Connorsville	AB	R	H	E
Dale, ss	5	2	1	0
Krupa, 1b	5	1	4	1
Pafko, cf	4	1	2	0
Worman, p	5	2	1	0
Sevals, 2b	4	1	0	0
R. Lipovsky, rf	4	2	1	0
Fennie, c	5	1	2	0

called Dunning Field for many years. In 2012, I challenged the city and the St. Paul School District to use the name Toni Stone Field on all of its schedules and other resources. Fortunately, St. Paul City Councilman Melvin Carter III directed the Parks and Recreation Department to use the name Toni Stone Field in the Dunning Complex. The school district responded in like manner. A new plaque was placed on the site in 2013.

Another young black ballplayer that Jimmy Lee highlighted in his "In the Sport Light" column was Johnny Walton Jr. In the April 23, 1937, issue of the *Spokesman*, Lee wrote that Walton "pitched remarkable ball last year" for Cretin High School. Walton had been the first African American student at Cretin, where he played baseball for four seasons (1935–38). Before that he had starred for the St. Andrews baseball team of the local parochial loop.

Three months after Lee's piece on Walton's accomplishments at Cretin, the *Spokesman* noted an upcoming appearance by Walton in the St. Paul Municipal Leagues for "Blue & White Cab, a team that should be in first place but is in second place because of some tough breaks received earlier

Jimmy Lee

JIMMY LEE was one of the leading African American sportswriters in the Twin Cities during the 1930s and '40s, chronicling the exploits of the area's black athletes at all levels. He was also a talented athlete and, later, one of the top sports officials—or "sports arbitrators," as Jim Griffin called him.

In addition to his baseball career with the Uptown Sanitary Shop and the Twin City Colored Giants, among others, Lee was an outstanding golfer, and he began his career with the *Minneapolis Spokesman* writing an article on golf tips, called "Golf Divots." Soon and for many years thereafter he was writing his "In the Sports Lights" column, keeping the community informed of highlights from local and some national athletes. (His column was also an invaluable resource for this book.)

Lee was one of the most sought-after and respected sports officials in Minnesota. During much of his officiating career, he was nearly always the only black person in the stadium or gym. His reputation first came to the attention of the University of Minnesota's head baseball coach, Dick Siebert. He hired Lee on a regular basis, making him the first black umpire to work in the Big Ten baseball conference. His efforts were so exemplary that he was also hired to work the National Collegiate Athletic Association regional baseball tournament.

When the Minnesota State High School League had a one-class basketball tournament, Lee worked in twenty of the thirty-two districts and six of the eight regions. Due to his race, however, he never had the honor of officiating in the state basketball tournament. Joe Hutton Sr., Hall of Famer and Hamline University basketball coach, called Jimmy Lee one of the finest basketball officials in the Midwest.

Johnny Walton Jr. (center) with the Cretin High School baseball team, 1936

In addition to working football, basketball, and baseball games for high schools and college, he also officiated in the Southern Minny baseball league. When Negro League teams barnstormed through Minnesota, Lee would work the games at the Lexington and Nicollet ballparks. As he traveled all over the state, Jimmy Lee was a fine ambassador for the black community. He was extremely popular, and it was common for Jimmy to be greeted by half the fans in the stands.

In 1972, Lee was inducted into the Minnesota Football Coaches Association Hall of Fame, the first black official to achieve this distinction. Paul Giel, former major league pitcher and Gopher athletic director, was the main speaker at the induction ceremony. When Jimmy was called to the podium to receive his plaque, the three-hundred-plus attendees rose to their feet in a standing ovation.

In 1974, the Oxford Recreation Center was renamed the Jimmy Lee Recreation Center. In the book *A Son of Rondo*, Jim Griffin shared that if anyone asks him "who was your hero?" the answer would be simple: "Without a moment's hesitation, my response would be 'Jimmy Lee!'"

I am proud to say that I worked with several people to get Jimmy Lee inducted into the Minnesota State High School League Hall of Fame in 2013, an honor long overdue. In remarks for the ceremony, Donald "Bill" McMoore, former athletic director for Minneapolis Public Schools, put it best: "Jimmy Lee . . . was not only a fine person and a real gentleman; he was also one of the finest football, basketball, and baseball officials Minnesota has ever seen." ●

in the season." Walton's name is also featured in a preview of an American Legion game just a few weeks after that: "Quite a pitchers battle is anticipated when the Leslie Lawrence and Johnny Baker teams meet for the American Legion Championship of the Twin Cities, August 16 at Harriet Island. It will be Johnny Walton, a corking good right hander for the Lawrence team, and Donald Strawder, a corking good left-hander for the Baker team."

Walton continued as a star pitcher in the local municipal leagues in 1938, and the following year he had a tryout with the Chicago American Giants of the Negro American League. After moving to California in 1945, he joined up with the San Francisco Sea Lions of the West Coast Negro Baseball League. Walton was later traded to the San Diego Tigers. The West Coast Negro Baseball League had been formed in March 1946 by two Berkeley firemen. Abe Saperstein, founder of the Harlem Globetrotters, was elected president, and Olympic track star Jessie Owens served as vice president. The league lasted only a short time, folding in July 1946.

As the decade of the 1930s was coming to a close, two teams—led by former teammates from the great Uptown Sanitary Shop clubs of the 1920s—would vie for the title of best black team in the Twin Cities. The Twin City Colored Giants, managed by George White, was the best known, having traveled throughout the region and into Canada to take on competitors. Dennis Ware managed the St. Paul–based Collins-Garrick team, another traveling squad, in 1938 and '39.

The Collins-Garrick club was sponsored by an establishment located at 365 Western Avenue in St. Paul, across the street from the Welcome Hall field (which later became the Ober Boys Club). Robert Collins and Louis Garrett took over the bar at this site in 1934; their business license was registered under the name Collins-Garrett, and it's unclear if the change to Collins-Garrick was simply the result of a typo somewhere along the way or if the name was changed deliberately. George Butler and Levi Garrett became the proprietors in 1936, and in 1946 Levi's wife, Effie Garrett, took over and ran the bar until 1957.

Back in the late 1930s, the Collins-Garrick baseball club held practices and hosted games at Welcome Hall field at Western and St. Anthony

Avenues, as well as at Dunning Field on Marshall Avenue and the Hollow Playground on the corner of Kent Street and St. Anthony Avenue. The Twin City Colored Giants also would sometimes practice and play at Welcome Hall field. From just across the street, patrons of the Collins-Garrick bar and pool hall were known to come out and watch the action on the field, and the bar was a popular gathering place after games as well.

Beyond the games in St. Paul's Rondo neighborhood, Ware's Collins-Garrick team (also referred to in the newspapers as the "C & G Rec." team) would travel outside the Twin Cities to play town ball teams in other areas of Minnesota and in Wisconsin. An article from the *Minneapolis Spokesman* in June 1939, about a game between Collins-Garrick and the team from Somerset, Wisconsin, mentioned "star twirler John Davis." An item in Lee's "In the Sport Light" column from July 14 described a game between the elite Twin Cities black teams of this era: "The Colored Giants again succeeded in beating the Collins-Garrick ball team, both teams having won 2 games. A rubber game will be played in the near future." The results of that tiebreaker have not been located.

Black Baseball Rosters of the 1930s

1930 COLORED HOUSE OF DAVID
From Todd Peterson, Early Black Baseball in Minnesota *(McFarland & Co., 2010)*

Ray Doan (manager)
Boldridge (3B/P)
Broadway (LF)
Campbell (P)
Dramar (2B)
Everett (SS)
Hamilton (1B)
Charlie Hancock (C/1B)
Hilton (2B/3B)
Jones (RF)
Neil (C)
Streets (CF)
Van (P)
Walton (3B)
Wilson (P)
Worley (LF)

1930 ST. PAUL COLORED GOPHERS

From Todd Peterson, Early Black Baseball in Minnesota *(McFarland & Co., 2010)*

Davis (C)
Farell (2B)
Gyden (RF)
Jackson (LF/P)
King (P/LF)
Lee (1B)
Robertson (SS)
Roosevelt (3B)
White (CF)

1931 COLORED HOUSE OF DAVID

From Todd Peterson, Early Black Baseball in Minnesota *(McFarland & Co., 2010)*

John Donaldson (P)
Bill Freeman (P)
Barker (CF/LF)
Boldridge (3B)
Everett (SS/C)
Gill (1B)
Hancock (1B)
Hilton (2B)
Jones (RF/LF/CF)
Porter (P/RF)
Streets (CF/2B/SS)
Truesdale (P)
Williams (C)
Wilson (RF)
Worley (LF)
Wright (LF/C)
Young (P/1B)

1932 JOHN DONALDSON ALL STARS (FAIRMONT, MN)

From Todd Peterson, Early Black Baseball in Minnesota *(McFarland & Co., 2010)*

John Donaldson (manager/P/CF/ LF)
J. Moore Allen (P/LF/RF)
Anderson
Buzz Boldridge (3B)
Joe "Jelly Roll" Barker (CF/3B/2B)
Cunningham (1B/C)
F. Sylvester "Hooks" Foreman (C)
Bill Freeman (P/CF)
Graves (1B)
Roosevelt "Chappie" Gray (1B/C)
Ham'lon (SS)
Charlie Hancock (SS/1B)
Robert "Piggy" Hawkins (3B/SS)
Charlie Hilton (2B/SS)
George Jones (P/RF/CF)
N. Jones (RF/LF)
McDonald (P/1B/RF)
Hurley McNair (LF/RF/CF/3B)
Smith (3B/SS)
Starks (2B/3B/1B/SS/OF)
Street (2B)
Worley (3B/SS)

1932 ST. PAUL MONARCHS

From Todd Peterson, Early Black Baseball in Minnesota; *additions from the July 23 edition of* Twin City Herald *indicated with an asterisk*

Frank Boyce (*owner)
Bedeau (SS)
Breedlove (RF)
Burke (PR)
Bill Coleman (3B)
*John Davis
Gerhard Dunlap (C)
Engles (CF)
Thomas English (CF)
Bill Johnson (SS)
"Rubber Arm" Johnson (OF/C)
Jimmy Lee (2B/1B)
Louis (2B)
Bobby Marshall (1B)
Victor McGowan (OF)
George Earl Roach (P)
Earl Thompson (P)
Vick (LF)

1934 MINNEAPOLIS COLORED GIANTS

From Todd Peterson, Early Black Baseball in Minnesota, *and May 19 edition of* Twin City Herald

Maceo Breedlove (RF)
Coleman (SS)
Lee Davis (C)
Tom English
Foot (2B)
Bill Freeman (P)

Harris (CF)
Jackson (LF)
K. Jackson (P)
Ollie (1B)
Vick (3B)

1935 MINNESOTA COLORED GOPHERS/ TWIN CITY COLORED GIANTS

From Todd Peterson, Early Black Baseball in Minnesota; *additions from the March 29 edition of the* Minneapolis Spokesman *indicated with an asterisk*

Jake Footes (manager/C/1B)
Maceo Breedlove (RF)
Carter (3B)
Wellington Coleman (2B/3B)
Tom English (SS)
Bill Freeman (1B)
Hamilton (SS)
Charles Hilton (2B)
Reggie Hopwood (CF)
Victor McGowan (LF/umpire)
Ollie Pettiford (1B)
"Lefty" Porter (P/LF)
E. N. Smith
Jean Thomas (P)
*Thompson (P)
Thorpe (P)
Gean Tucker
John Van (C)
Dennis Ware (C)
Robert Wethers
Chink Worley (1B/LF)

1935 MINNEAPOLIS KEYSTONE TIGERS
From the August 16 edition of the Minneapolis Spokesman

Bill Brooks (manager)
Gene Harris (assistant)

1935 LESLIE LAWRENCE AMERICAN LEGION JUNIOR TEAM (YOUTH BASEBALL)
From the May 17 edition of the Minneapolis Spokesman

Claude Collins
Willis Clark
John Henry Cyrus
John Davis
Readus Fletcher
Sam Howell
Harold K. Howland
Matthew Johnson
Roger Johnson
James G. Kirk
Stephen Maxwell
William Edward Robinson
Chas. Alden Russell
Edwin Smith
Lonnie Washington

1936 ST. PAUL GOPHERS
From the August 15 edition of the Twin City Herald

Flash (SS)
Footes (C)
Johnson (RF)
Oler (1B)
Roach (LF)
Taylor (3B)
Thompson (P)
Wakeoff (P)
White (CF)
Worley (2B)

1937 ST. PAUL COLORED GIANTS
From the April 16 edition of the Minneapolis Spokesman

Jake Footes (C)
Guyden (utility)
F. Johnson (SS)
J. Johnson (RF)
Jimmy Lee (2B)
Martin (utility)
Lefty Oller (LF)
T. Porter (1B/P)
George Roach (P)
"Toni" Stone (P)
Worley (3B)
Wakoff (P)
George White (manager/CF)

1937 PHYLLIS WHEATLEY HOUSE CARDINALS TEAM (MINNEAPOLIS)

From Todd Peterson, Early Black Baseball in Minnesota *(McFarland & Co., 2010)*

Sylvester Carter (coach)

Minzie Davis (P/OF)

Donald Strawder (P/OF)

Bill Freeman (P)

Billy Roach (P)

Ed Jackson (C)

Burton Lewis (C)

Stafford Lott (infield)

Red Martin (infield)

Leroy Reese (infield)

Everett Vaughn (infield)

Donald Sessions (infield)

Barnell Breedlove (infield)

Charles Miller (infield)

Ward Bell (OF)

Cozwell Breedlove (OF)

Larry "Bubba" Brown (OF)

1938 COLLINS-GARRICK

From the June 16 edition of the Minneapolis Spokesman

Dennis Ware (manager)

English (CF)

Foster (LF)

Harroway (3B)

Howe (RF)

Johnson (SS)

Perry (1B)

Roach (P)

Smith (C)

Thomas (2B)

1938 TWIN CITY COLORED GIANTS

From the September 7 edition of the Dunn County News

Worley (SS)

Vickes (2B)

White (LF)

Davis (3B)

T. Jackson (CF)

Ford (1B)

Guyden (RF)

E. Jackson (C)

Richardson (P)

Roach (P)

Tom Boy (Toni) Stone (LF)

1939 COLLINS-GARRICK

From the June 1939 edition of the Minneapolis Spokesman

Dennis Ware (manager)

John Davis (P)

"Sammy" Howell (P)

·5·
The 1940s
The End of the Color Barrier in Organized Baseball— But Barriers Still Exist

BY THE DAWN OF THE 1940S, the United States had climbed its way out of the darkest days of the Great Depression—thanks in large part to President Franklin Roosevelt's New Deal programs and to the outbreak of World War II, which boosted industry with the global demand for war-related materials. When the United States entered the war following the attack on Pearl Harbor in December 1941, the need for workers increased dramatically, not only because of the further demands on industrial production but also because many able-bodied men had enlisted in the armed forces, creating new vacancies on the home front.

Some companies opened their doors to African American workers, particularly after President Roosevelt issued Executive Order 8802, which banned discrimination in "the employment of workers in defense industries and in government," in June 1941. Many businesses perpetuated their discriminatory policies, however, and African Americans continued to struggle to find work beyond menial positions that brought little or no potential for advancement.

Organizations such as the Urban League and the NAACP were active in Minnesota, as elsewhere, during the 1940s, fighting discrimination and injustice in all areas of life, from housing and employment to where black people could eat or shop. The April 12, 1940, issue of the *Minneapolis Spokesman* gave front-page coverage to Governor Harold Stassen's praise

Discrimination Must Cease in Defense Program!

EVERY LOYAL CITIZEN who is interested in securing equal rights for all citizens in the defense program of the State and Nation is invited to attend this... **CITIZENS' MASS MEETING.**

—— WE WANT ——

Your Cooperation in Securing EQUAL RIGHTS FOR THE NEGRO in the MINNESOTA HOME DEFENSE FORCE *and in the...* **Industrial Units of the State and National Defense Program.** We Urge You to Meet us at the

PHYLIS WHEATLEY HOUSE

809 Aldrich Avenue North, Minneapolis

SUNDAY, JUNE 1, 1941

——AT 4 O'CLOCK P. M.——

The Minnesota NEGRO DEFENSE Committee

FRANK L. ALSUP, Chairman   JAMES L. HOWLAND, Secretary
JAMES SLEMMONS, Vice Chairman   JOSE SHERWOOD, Treasurer
REV. CLARENCE T. R. NELSON, Publicity Chairman

for the Urban League's work against racial injustice during that organization's annual dinner. The NAACP also led numerous protests to fight discrimination and Jim Crow policies in the Twin Cities.

In addition to the changing landscape at home, America's entry into World War II brought to a head the issue of segregation and discrimination in the nation's armed forces. Many African Americans were committed to supporting their country in the fight for freedom and justice overseas, and thousands joined up right away, despite being denied basic rights at home. According to the National WWII Museum, more than a million African American men and women served in the armed forces during the course of the war, either at home or abroad. The military remained fully segregated, however, and, as on the home front, most African Americans were relegated to support and logistical roles. But some all-black combat units distinguished themselves in battle, most notably the Tuskegee Airmen and the 761st Tank Battalion. This valuable service ultimately led President Harry S. Truman to desegregate the armed services with Executive Order 9981, issued on July 26, 1948, guaranteeing equal "treatment and opportunity for all persons in the armed services without regard to race, color, religion or national origin."

President Truman's act to desegregate the military—an arm of the U.S. federal government—was a landmark moment in the civil rights movement. And it came nearly three years after Branch Rickey desegregated organized baseball with the signing of Jackie Robinson to a minor league contract in October 1945, and more than a year after Robinson became the first African American to appear in a major league game, on April 15, 1947.

One of the ironies of the long-awaited integration of Major League Baseball is that it ultimately led to the demise of the organized Negro Leagues. The Negro Leagues had provided many more opportunities to African Americans for both employment and business ownership than the

Poster for anti-discrimination rally at the Phyllis Wheatley House on June 1, 1941, shortly before President Franklin Roosevelt issued an executive order banning discrimination in the defense program. Minnesota Historical Society Collections

majors would ever offer. As Bob Kendrick, president of the Negro Leagues Baseball Museum in Kansas City, put it, while the signing of black players into the majors was "a tremendous occasion, it was the beginning of the end for what was known as Negro League baseball. It was devastating to black-owned businesses that supported Negro Leagues baseball, such as hotels, restaurants, and other service businesses."

Nevertheless, during the 1940s, the Negro National League and the Negro American League continued to attract elite black athletes. Local clubs and barnstorming teams offered additional opportunities for black ballplayers to play the game they loved. Others headed to Canada, where they could earn a living playing in integrated leagues north of the border.

Most of the all-black teams in Minnesota remained part-time pursuits for players who, as in previous decades, had to work during the week to earn a living, fitting in practices in the evenings and games on the weekends or holidays. Long gone were the days, from around the turn of the twentieth century, when teams like the St. Paul Colored Gophers or the Minneapolis Keystones could accept challenges every chance they got and make money while barnstorming.

The leading black teams of the early 1940s remained the clubs skippered by former players Dennis Ware and George White. The Collins-Garrick (also known as C & G Recreation) team and the Twin City Colored Giants set the standard for black baseball in the Twin Cities.

C & G Recreation kicked off its 1940 season in the St. Paul City League with "their first game Saturday, May 12 against the strong Northern Envelope team, last year known as the J. J. Kohns and Champions of the league two years previous," according to the *Minneapolis Spokesman* of April 26. "The game will be played on Como #1. Managers Ware and [John] Walton [Sr.] have not announced their battery yet, but it's almost a lead pipe cinch that Johnny Walton, a veteran in City League competition, and 'Foots' McCray will get the nod." The May 17 newspaper reported a 12–10 loss for C & G Recreation, whose next game was scheduled for May 18 against the Milk Driver's United team at Lexington Park.

Veteran catcher Jake "Foots" McCray was a cornerstone of the C & G team. Jimmy Lee named McCray athlete of the week in his "Sport Light" column of May 24, 1940, citing McCray's prowess both at the plate and behind it: "Jake (Foots) McCray, veteran catcher for the C and G team, banged out four hits in four trips, one was a long homerun, plus handled pitcher Johnny Walton."

Two years later, a *Spokesman* article from May 8, 1942, still had Dennis Ware's C & G Recreation baseball team relying on youth in its lineup, which consisted of "Stanley Tabor at first, Rosby at second, Cotton at shortstop, Lloyd Gamble or Percy Hughes at third base, Worley, Jones, Stone and Breedlove outfield. Jones, who is now pitching for Mechanic Arts [High School] will join after school is out, Billy Marshall may be signed to hurl as soon as he drops the boxing gloves, veteran Jake Footes will catch."

The Twin City Colored Giants, meanwhile, continued to play all over the five-state area and Canada. The team was still managed by George White, who, like Ware, looked to the young players coming out of the municipal youth leagues to bolster his roster. On April 21, 1944, White announced, in the *Spokesman*, the start of spring training for the Twin City Giants, inviting calls by interested players.

White's Giants participated in a milestone of sorts in June 1946, when they took on the Nickel Joint Nine, "one of the strongest triple A clubs in the Northwest," at Lexington Park. According to Jimmy Lee's column in the *Spokesman*, "Twin City baseball fans will be treated to their first night baseball game featuring a Negro nine on Tuesday night, June 18, when the Twin City Colored Giants go to bat with the Nickel Joint Nine." The Giants' battery for the game was Sammy Harris, formerly

John Cotton, unknown player, and Lloyd "DuLov" Hogan of the Twin City Colored Gophers, circa 1945

of the Birmingham Black Barons, and "the reliable Jake Foots." George White, the article continued, "promises baseball fans several more attractive games during the season."

Some of those attractive games took place later that month and in early July in Port Williams and Port Arthur, Canada, where the Giants won four of five games. "The last game played in the five days they were in Canada was a 4–4 tie in 12 innings. Stanley Tabor hit a home run and Lefty, the pitcher, made 15 strikeouts." The *Spokesman* article also mentioned "hometown boy" Harold "Babe" Price, who, "after auditioning with TCCG'S, was found to be a close runner-up to Lefty, and will pitch for the Giants in the future."

On Friday, July 19, 1946, the Colored Giants took on the Midway All-Stars at Lexington Park. According to the pregame report, "McKensie or Price and White" would form the battery against the All-Stars, who are "very tough opponents."

During the 1940s, teams from the organized Negro Leagues regularly traveled to Minnesota on barnstorming tours. Barnstorming provided the players with an additional occasion to earn money at a time when it was difficult for them to make a decent living playing ball. Barnstorming also gave these ballplayers a chance to show off their skills and compete against talented clubs—white or black—in different locations. Minnesota was a popular destination, and the arrival of the visiting teams gave the local clubs and towns a chance to bring in some extra money as well. The typical arrangement was for the winner to get 60 percent of the gate, with 40 percent going to the losing team, regardless of who was the host team.

Abe Saperstein, best known as the owner of the Harlem Globetrotters basketball team, was also a promoter of black baseball in the 1930s and '40s. At various times, he had ownership stakes in the Cincinnati (later Indianapolis) Ethiopian Clowns, the Birmingham Black Barons, and the Chicago American Giants. He brought some of his teams to Minnesota on barnstorming tours.

In July 1940, Jimmy Lee's "In the Sport Light" column in the *Spokesman* noted a game between the Ethiopian Clowns and Cincinnati Hawkeyes: "We believe their shadow baseball game is the best we have seen in sometime, and we believe the three thousand people who attended the game will agree. . . . This team, although called the Clowns, carries everything a good baseball team should. Yes, they do clown, but they also play ball, and how!" Later that summer, the Ethiopian Clowns defeated the vaunted Kansas City Monarchs and their star pitcher Hilton Smith in front of three thousand fans in St. Paul.

As suggested by the team's name, it was not uncommon for "clowning" to be a part of the act for traveling black teams, and some (white) organizers viewed the men as entertainers more than serious baseball players. This expectation sometimes led to trouble when the "clowns" defeated the hometown team, and the visitors were chased out of town without pay.

Although Minnesota offered a more hospitable environment for black players than many areas of the country, and some players—such as Reggie Hopwood and John Donaldson—even settled here after visiting on barnstorming trips, the realities of racial discrimination and segregation were ever-present challenges for these traveling teams. Simply finding places to eat, hotels to get a good night's sleep, or service stations to fill up the gas tank were formidable, constant obstacles.

A vital resource for any African American traveling through the country during the era of Jim Crow was the *Negro Motorist Green Book*. First published in 1936 as a guide to travel in the New York City area, the book was soon expanded to cover most of the United States and parts of Canada and Mexico as well. The *Green Book* provided information and details on black-friendly businesses and accommodations in a given town or city, everything from hotels and restaurants to tailors and barbershops. The introduction to the 1948 edition explains the guide's goal of providing "the Negro traveler information that will keep him from running into difficulties, embarrassments and to make his trips more enjoyable."

While the editors of the book acknowledged that it was not comprehensive and that there were "thousands of places" they were unaware of when compiling the guide, the 1940 edition of the *Green Book* listed just one hotel in Minneapolis (the Serville, at 246½ 4th Avenue South) and one restaurant in St. Paul (G & G Bar-B-Q at 318 Rondo Street). At the end of the decade, the Serville remained the only Minnesota hotel listed,

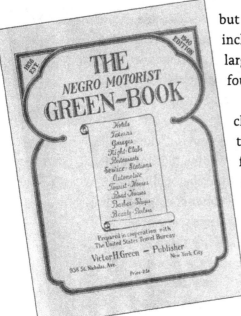

but several additional restaurants and taverns were included for the Twin Cities in the 1949 edition. The largest number of "Negro-friendly" businesses were found under "Liquor Stores."

Based on what Buck O'Neil, "Double Duty" Radcliffe, and many other former players have reported, traveling baseball was not particularly glamorous for African Americans in the 1940s; instead, it was fraught with challenges and dangers. Their stories and recollections make me think about my own father and his safety as he traveled to play the game he loved and to earn some additional money to support his young family.

◆　◆　◆

On October 23, 1945, Branch Rickey, the president and general manager of the Brooklyn Dodgers, signed Jackie Robinson to a baseball contract. A four-sport collegiate star at UCLA (baseball, basketball, football, and track), Robinson had just completed a season with the Kansas City Monarchs of the Negro American League. Rickey announced that Robinson would play for the Montreal Royals, a Dodgers farm team in the International League, for the 1946 season. Rickey was the first baseball executive willing to openly challenge Major League Baseball's policy of segregation, which had been in effect for more than fifty years.

Robinson spent one season with the Royals—and led the International League with a .349 average—and then went to Cuba to join the Dodgers for spring training in February 1947. There, a young white player from St. Paul, Howie Schultz, became Robinson's mentor and showed him the ropes for playing first base. (Robinson's normal position was second base, but the Dodgers already had all-star Eddie Stanky at that position.)

On April 10, the Dodgers announced they were purchasing Robinson from Montreal so that he could join the major league roster. Five days later, in the Dodgers' opening game of the 1947 season, Jackie Robinson trotted onto the field as Brooklyn's starting first baseman, officially breaking the color barrier in Major League Baseball. Less than a month later, the Dodgers sold Schultz to the Phillies for $50,000.

Skip Schultz, Howie's son, recalled a story that his father had told him about the Dodgers' first trip to Philadelphia to play the Phillies that season. (This story is particularly special to me because Howie Schultz became an important influence on my life as my coach in basketball and baseball during high school.) Philadelphia manager Ben Chapman (who grew up in Alabama) was one of the most virulent and outspoken opponents to Robinson's presence in the majors. In the first inning of the Sunday game in Philadelphia, Phillies pitcher Schoolboy Rowe hit Robinson with his first pitch. As Jackie picked himself up off the dirt and trotted to first base, the Philadelphia crowd and the players in the Phillies dugout showered him with racial slurs. When Robinson arrived at first base, Philadelphia first baseman Howie Schultz asked him, "Jackie, how do you take this day after day?" Jackie responded, "It's okay, Howie. I'll have my day."

Have his day, he did. Not only would Robinson go on to win Rookie of the Year honors in 1947, he maintained a ten-year Hall of Fame career in the major leagues.

Even after the landmark signing and Robinson's star-caliber play on the field, the floodgates of opportunity did not open for African Americans in major league baseball. In testimony before the House Un-American Activities Committee in July 1949, Robinson noted:

> I'm not fooled because I've had a chance open to very few Negro Americans. It's true that I've been the laboratory specimen in a great change in organized baseball. I'm proud that I've made good on my assignment to the point where other colored players will find it easier to enter the game and go to the top. But I'm well aware that even this limited job isn't finished yet. There are only three major league clubs with only seven colored players signed up, out of close to four hundred major league players on sixteen clubs.

Many teams held off for years before signing any black players. Even for forward-thinking owners like Branch Rickey, Horace Stoneham of the New York Giants, and Bill Veeck of the Cleveland Indians, the number of black players on their rosters was limited by a kind of unofficial quota system. Giving spots to African Americans was viewed as taking jobs away from white players.

Veeck, a true baseball maverick for his promotional savvy, was the second owner to cross the sport's long-standing policy of segregation. Larry Doby signed with Veeck's Cleveland Indians on July 5, 1947, making him the first black player in the American League. Doby had made his professional baseball debut with the Newark Eagles of the Negro National League in 1942, when he was just eighteen years old, and he remained with that team until Veeck came calling. Whereas Rickey paid no compensation to the Kansas City Monarchs when he plucked Robinson out of the Negro Leagues, Newark owner Effa Manley insisted that Veeck buy out Doby's contract. In the end, he paid Manley $15,000 for Doby, who would play thirteen seasons in the majors and earn induction into the National Baseball Hall of Fame.

Later in July of '47, Hank Thompson made his debut with the lowly St. Louis Browns of the American League. He played only 27 games that season and then was released by St. Louis. Thompson returned to the Kansas City Monarchs, where he had played prior to the Browns. The New York Giants then signed him before the 1949 season. His debut with the Giants on July 8, 1949, made Thompson the only player to break the color barrier for two different teams. (Former Newark Eagle Monte Irvin also pinch-hit for the Giants later in that same game.)

During the 1940s and '50s, the Minneapolis Millers served as a Giants' farm team, and Thompson would spend time in the Twin Cities during brief minor league stints in 1951 and 1957. Irvin played part of the 1955 season with the Millers.

While Thompson, Irvin, and another up-and-coming star in the Giants organization, Willie Mays, all played for the Millers in Minneapolis during the 1950s, across the river the St. Paul Saints were a minor league affiliate for the Dodgers. After earning distinction as the first black *pitcher* in the major leagues—when he took the mound for Brooklyn against the Pittsburgh Pirates on August 26, 1947—Dan Bankhead joined the Saints during the 1948 season. Bankhead's teammate behind the plate in St. Paul that year was another future major league star: Roy Campanella.

Roy Campanella of the St. Paul Saints, shaking hands with manager Walter Alston as he heads for home after hitting a home run at Nicollet Park against the Minneapolis Millers, May 31, 1948. Minnesota Historical Society Collections

Campanella's arrival in St. Paul in the spring of 1948, as the first African American player in the American Association, was highly anticipated. As the *Minneapolis Spokesman* reported on May 28, "St. Paul will be the first city in the American Association Baseball League to have a Negro American player on its roster."

Because the first-place Saints already had strong players behind the plate in '48, the new young catcher was going to have to battle for playing time, and Campanella's first few games were not as productive as had been expected. According to the *Minneapolis Spokesman*, "His lack of play within the past few weeks probably has some effect on his ability to hit at this stage."

But Campanella soon launched a torrid hitting spree—which all but assured that his stay in St. Paul would be brief. In 35 games with the St. Paul Saints, he posted impressive statistics: .325 batting average, 13 home runs, 39 runs batted in, and a slugging percentage of .715. By July 2, 1948, he was wearing a Brooklyn Dodgers uniform. By July 12, 1949, he was making the first of what would be eight consecutive appearances in the major league all-star game. (Joining Campy in the 1949 Midsummer Classic were Dodger teammates Jackie Robinson and Don Newcombe and Cleveland's Larry Doby as the first African Americans to play in an MLB all-star game.)

No hotels in St. Paul at this time allowed blacks, so Campanella stayed with sportswriter Jimmy Griffin when he first arrived in Minnesota in 1948. Then, like many others, he boarded at the Rideaux home on Rondo Street. The Price family lived across the street from the boardinghouse, and Verlene (Price) Booker shared the following story: "Every time Mr. Campanella hit a homerun, they [General Mills] would give him a case of Wheaties, and he would bring the case back to the Rideaux's. They would give Wheaties to all the neighbors, because Roy wasn't going to eat all that cereal." This generosity defined the Rondo community—people were always looking out for others, helping when they could.

A year after Campanella and Bankhead played in St. Paul, the Minneapolis Millers signed their first black players. The *Spokesman* reported on the arrival of Ray Dandridge and Dave Barnhill in the June 10, 1949, paper:

Millers Buy Two Negro Players to Strengthen Team

Barnhill and Dandridge Stars of New York Cubans Flown Here

The Minneapolis Millers became the second team in the American Association to open its roster to Negro-American players Sunday when David Barnhill and Ray Dandridge of the New York Cubans joined the Mill City team.

Barnhill, a highly touted pitcher, and Dandridge, a second baseman, [were] purchased Saturday by manager Rosy Ryan for an undisclosed amount which was said to run into several figures.

Minneapolis Millers Ray Dandridge, Dave Barnhill, and Willie Mays. National Baseball Hall of Fame Library, Cooperstown, New York

Already thirty-five years old in 1949 following an eight-year Negro League career, Barnhill played three seasons with the Millers at Nicollet Park, posting an overall win-loss record of 24–18, but he never got the call to the major leagues. Dandridge, also a thirty-five-year-old "rookie" with the Millers in '49, batted .318 and hit 37 homers in four seasons in Minneapolis. He would earn induction into the Baseball Hall of Fame for his stellar Negro League career, primarily with the Newark Eagles.

Back on the other side of the river, the St. Paul Saints signed Jim Pendleton from the Chicago American Giants in 1949. The outfielder spent three seasons with the Saints before eventually moving up to the majors in 1953.

The end of World War II in August 1945 had led to a great influx of baseball talent throughout the sport. In the book *Town Ball*, Armand Peterson and Tom Tomashek note that this resurgence was very evident in Minnesota. "Returning servicemen flooded the state," they wrote, "and almost 250 new teams started up. The renaissance was widespread."

This renaissance had a less dramatic impact on Minnesota's black community. Because the Association of Minnesota Amateur Baseball Leagues still enforced a ban on African Americans, an increase in the number of teams did not bring new opportunities for black players, at least not for a few more years.

Ben Sternberg, a boxing promoter from Rochester, Minnesota, was an important figure in bringing black players to Minnesota in the latter half of the 1940s. According to Peterson and Tomashek, Sternberg had developed a friendship with Abe Saperstein, the Harlem Globetrotters owner and an active promoter of Negro League baseball. Among the players recommended to Sternberg by Saperstein was pitcher Gread "Lefty" McKinnis.

McKinnis had been an emerging star with Saperstein's Birmingham Black Barons and Chicago American Giants in the Negro American League during the first half of the decade, and he had a sensational first season with the Rochester Queens in 1947, playing in the Southeastern Minnesota League. McKinnis posted a 26–4 record overall and averaged 16 strikeouts per game. He pitched the Queens to a 1–0 victory in the semifinals of the Class A State Tournament—allowing only two hits and providing the game's only scoring with a home run of his own—but he got the loss in the final game, played the next day. McKinnis was named the most valuable player of the Class A tournament. His performance reopened the door to black players in the state tournament.

McKinnis pitched for Sternberg's Queens again in 1948 but then returned to the Chicago American Giants in 1949. Still, Rochester had

Gread "Lefty" McKinnis

several black players on its roster in '49. Now known as the Rochester Royals (following a merger of two Rochester teams) and playing in the Southern Minnesota League, Sternberg's club featured Marlin "Mel" Carter, Sam Hill, and Sam "Red" Jones. Both Carter and Hill had played for Saperstein's American Giants in 1948. Jones, also known as "Toothpick Sam," had pitched for the Cleveland Buckeyes of the Negro American League in 1947 and '48. He won twelve games for Rochester in 1949, including a no-hitter, and then was signed by the Cleveland Indians prior to the 1950 season on his way to a twelve-year career in the majors. Despite its strong team, Rochester lost in the playoffs of the Southern Minny and failed to advance to the state tournament in 1949.

Over in Fulda in southwest Minnesota, local businessmen and baseball boosters Dick Reusse and George Rauenhorst went to Kansas City to recruit players for the Fulda Giants. They signed Hilton Smith, the legendary Kansas City Monarchs pitcher and future Hall of Famer. Smith was in his forties at the time, but he helped raise interest in the local ball club, which reached the Class A State Tournament in 1949. The Giants also signed Cuban-born Earl Ashby, another pitcher and former Negro Leaguer, late in the season.

Other small-town Minnesota teams soon began signing veterans and young stars from the ranks of black ball as well. These players often jumped from town to town in search of new opportunity and better pay. As Peterson and Tomashek note, "Very few of those signed in 1949 played out the season [with the same team] or returned in 1950."

Still, the options for black players remained limited. By the time of integration, players who had established successful careers in the Negro Leagues were often too old to receive serious consideration from major league organizations. Some, like McKinnis, did sign minor league contracts but were used primarily to fill out rosters. And as organized baseball plucked off more and more of the top young talent from black communities around the country, the Negro Leagues faced a rapid decline. The Negro National League folded after the 1948 season. The Negro American League hung on as a legitimate entity until 1950, but through the rest of the decade it operated more at the level of semipro or amateur ball. Consequently, men like McKinnis and others returned to barnstorming black teams and integrated semipro leagues to find baseball jobs.

Another new direction for black players at the time was the rise of softball, or "kitten ball" as it was then known. Many athletes who had played baseball began trying out for softball. Earl Cannon managed a team in St. Paul that featured the following roster: Al Harris and Don Taylor (catchers), Simmy Scroggins and James Toliver (pitchers), Littleton Gardner (1B), Otis Skinner and Andrew Hartshorn (right-SS), Stanley Tabor (left-SS), Lawrence Wycoff (2B), Peter Buford (3B), George Cummings (CF), Bobby Jones (LF), Cleveland Ray (RF), and Manley Rhodes and Tommy English (utility).

◆ ◆ ◆

Many local black athletes made names for themselves playing baseball during the 1940s. One of the best is relatively unknown today but is mentioned by many who recall seeing him play. Harold "Babe" Price was a star pitcher with various local outfits, yet there is scant record of his performances on the diamond.

The Price family was originally from Lincoln, Nebraska, where Harold was born, and they later moved to St. Paul. Harold Price's name doesn't appear in accounts of city high school baseball or any of the youth teams. According to his sister Verlene Price Booker, he was enrolled at an occupational school on the city's west side but wasn't much interested in school. Known to many as "Babe," Harold went fishing every chance he got—likely skipping classes and neglecting his schoolwork. Verlene said he dropped out at age sixteen and eventually enlisted in the U.S. Navy.

The first written evidence of Babe Price as a baseball player appears in the *Minneapolis Spokesman* on July 12, 1946, where he was named as a member of the Twin City Colored Giants. The frequent catcher for Price, according to various articles about the Colored Giants, was Louis White, my father.

The Colored Giants traveled all over Minnesota, along the St. Croix River Valley, into Wisconsin, and up to Canada—anyplace they could find a worthy opponent. A newspaper clipping from the *Dunn County News* on June 25, 1947—located by Matt Carter at the Dunn County Historical Society in Menomonie, Wisconsin—described a game between the Colored Giants and the Wakanda Braves of Menomonie earlier that month. The article tells of the Braves' thrilling 8–7 extra-inning victory over the Giants—"one of the best games of the current baseball season"—in which "Price, Giants hurler, mowed down 22 Braves by way of the strikeout route." (I later learned, from the original scorebook also located by Matt Carter, that my father was in the lineup for the Colored Giants that day.)

In July 1948, Price and the Giants traveled to Winnipeg for a six-game series over three days. In the series, Price and teammate Solomon Drake played well enough to be signed by the Elmwood Giants of the Manitoba Senior Baseball League.

According to Lacey Curry—a member of the St. Paul Saints from 1956 to 1960 and a friend of Solomon Drake's—"Solly" had been recruited by George White as a high schooler in Little Rock, Arkansas, when he was just seventeen years old. This story illustrates White's far-reaching recruitment efforts for the Colored Giants. Drake would go on to bat .300 with Elmwood in 1950, and in early 1951 he was signed by the Chicago Cubs. He played a few years in the Cubs' minor league system before spending time with the big league club in 1956. He was purchased by the Dodgers that same year and played for their St. Paul Saints affiliate, leading the club with a .333 average.

Price, who went by "Hal" (rather than Babe) in Canada, appeared in six games for Elmwood in 1948 after being signed in July. He completed all five of his starts but ended with an overall record of 1–5. Price did well the following season, going 14–8 in 31 games played and completing 17 of his 18 starts. He spent most of the season with Elmwood but finished out the year with the Brandon Greys, also of the Manitoba Senior Baseball League.

In the season-opening doubleheader between the Giants and the Greys on May 21, 1949, Price struck out twelve batters and allowed seven hits in the nightcap, but his Giants lost the game. About two thousand fans were in attendance.

Later that season, on August 9 and 10, Price went up against fellow St. Paul transplant Toni Stone, then playing for the New Orleans Creoles.

Stone appeared in three innings of the Creoles' 10–6 victory in the opener. The Giants won the following day, 15–5, with Price playing outfield and collecting three hits in the contest. Stone played just one inning. Although Price never pitched against Stone, one might imagine a lively conversation about playing for the Twin City Colored Giants in St. Paul, which Stone had done several years before Price.

The Brandon Greys completed the 1949 season with a remarkable record of 87 wins, 18 losses, and 3 ties. Price was responsible for three Greys losses after joining the team late in the season, including two in the league playoffs in August.

On April 14, 1950, the *Winnipeg Free Press* reported that the Elmwood Giants had signed Clyde Golden, "left-handed Negro pitcher, who it is hoped will make up for the loss of Hal Price, Negro ace who starred with the club for two seasons before signing a contract with the Brooklyn Dodgers." Unfortunately, Price's career with the Dodgers never got off the ground. During spring training at Vero Beach, Florida, Price was shot in the knee while attempting to assist someone in a brawl.

George White's Boardinghouse and Gambling Emporium

JOE RAY WAS A MEMBER of George White's Twin City Colored Giants, and he was also a close friend of my father, Lou White. Joe explained that George's home—located at 348 North Kent Street, between Rondo and St. Anthony Avenues, across the alley from Jim Williams's bar—was a gathering place for players and included rooms upstairs for players' lodging.

When he recruited players from other parts of the country, like Solomon Drake from Arkansas, White often let them stay at his house during the season, either at little expense or perhaps as part of the player's contract. The main floor of his home was used for socializing and eating meals. But the basement was White's money-maker—what we would call an "after-hours place," where people gathered for a drink after the bars closed and to join in a poker game or maybe throw dice. The gambling was a way for George to raise some extra money to cover the team's expenses and to pay his players.

I remember one time, when I was about eleven or twelve years old, I went with my father to George's house. My father knocked, and a man opened the door slightly. He said, "Oh, it's you, Pud. Here," and he handed something to my father. I guess it was money he owed him for playing baseball. After we left, I asked my father, "Who was that man?" My father said it was coach George White. I asked if he was a relative. "No," he replied, "he's my coach on the baseball team." ●

His major league hopes dashed, Price returned to Canada and played with a barnstorming team from Sceptre, Saskatchewan, in 1950 and '51. Tournaments were a big deal in Western Canada, and Sceptre was one of the best tournament teams. According to the "Western Canada Baseball" website, the Sceptre team won a reported $17,000 in prize money during the 1950 season. They then won six tournaments in 1951, including the Western Canada semipro baseball championship sponsored by the National Baseball Congress. Price pitched back-to-back complete-game victories against the Indian Head Rockets to secure the title. Earlier that summer he had been selected as the all-star pitcher of the Medicine Hat tournament.

Price pitched two more seasons for Winnipeg-based teams in the ManDak League, which had formed in 1950 with four teams from Manitoba and one team from North Dakota. Price led the league with ten wins in 1952. Former Negro League legend Ted "Double Duty" Radcliffe was Price's player-manager for part of that season.

During the early 1950s, many black players headed north for jobs in the Canadian professional and semipro leagues. Among the former Negro League stars who spent their waning playing days in Canada were Radcliffe, Willie Wells, Lyman Bostock Sr., Chet Brewer, Leon Day, Gentry Jessup, Lester Lockett, Gread McKinnis, and others; even Satchel Paige pitched briefly for the Minot (ND) Mallards of the ManDak League. Also playing in Western Canada in 1950 were three men who would go on to become the first black players for three major league franchises:

Hal "Babe" Price and the Sceptre, Saskatchewan, baseball team

Tom Alston (St. Louis Cardinals), Pumpsie Green (Boston Red Sox), and John Kennedy (Philadelphia Phillies). Cecil Littles from St. Paul played for the Estevan Maple Leafs of the Western Canada League in 1951.

Price's last season was 1953, with the Winnipeg Royals. Why Price, still only twenty-seven years old, gave up the game at this point is unclear—

especially considering the vast opportunities in Canada for him to pursue his second great passion: fishing.

While Price made it with various professional and semipro teams around the region, others thrived on the local scene. John Cotton, a graduate of St. Paul's Marshall Senior High School in 1943, started playing for Dennis Ware on the C & G Rec team when he was only fourteen years old. "I remember learning the game from the older players," Cotton said, "the swing bunt or a delayed steal. These things helped me when I played in high school." He was an outstanding athlete at Marshall and earned all-city honors nine times, including selections for baseball, basketball, and football.

In addition to C & G, Cotton spent time playing for the Twin City Colored Gophers (later the Twin City Colored Giants). A phenomenal three-sport athlete in high school, Cotton went on to attend Louisville Municipal College in Kentucky to play football for coach Dwight Reed, who recruited a number of players from Minnesota. (Reed later coached several Minnesotans during his long tenure at Missouri's Lincoln University as well.)

Stanley Tabor, another outstanding multisport athlete of this era, was a teammate of Cotton's on Ware's C & G team and in both high school and college. He played first base for C & G Recreation. He was a star athlete at Marshall High School. After serving in the army, Cotton attended Louisville Municipal College and received numerous awards in baseball, basketball, football, golf, and bowling.

Along with Marshall Senior High School, St. Paul's Mechanic Arts High was another destination for young black athletes of the day. When the St. Paul City Conference celebrated its one-hundredth anniversary in 1999, it named the top one hundred male student-athletes from its first century. Among those so honored was Louis "Pud" White—my father. During his high school years at Mechanic Arts, he was named to all-city teams in three sports (baseball, basketball, and football), and in his final high school season in 1946, he won the conference batting title with a torrid .600 average, considered to this day the conference record.

As discussed in the introduction to this book, further endorsement

Portrait of Louis "Pud" White and a newspaper clipping from his record-setting 1946 season at Mechanic Arts High School (shown with pitcher Chuck Andresen)

Stars Talk It Over

Chuck Andresen, left, leading pitcher of the 1946 City prep baseball race shows Louis White, the conference top hitter, some of his tricks as the star Mechanic Arts battery gets together. Andresen won his sixth straight game of the season Monday as he beat Monroe, 6-2, while White is the No. 1 hitter with a sensational .600 average. The Trainers met Washington for the playoff title this afternoon at Dunning.

of "Pud" White's skills on the baseball diamond came from none other than the great Negro Leaguer Buck O'Neil, who had tried to recruit White out of high school to play for the Kansas City Monarchs. In a 2004 interview, Kwame McDonald asked O'Neil if the great Double Duty Radcliffe would throw a special pitch when facing White. Buck replied, "Double Duty would knock Lou White down! 'Cause Lou White could hit, man!"

My father once told me that the New York Yankees had come calling, but he didn't sign. In one of the few conversations he had with me about his baseball experiences, he claimed, "I would have been before Elston Howard" (the first black player on the Yankees). I don't have anything to substantiate this assertion—but my father didn't share lies.

After baseball began to fade in the black community of the Twin Cities, White starred on several fast-pitch softball teams in St. Paul and Minneapolis. His first team was for the Ted Bies Liquors store, which was made up of players who used to be on all-black baseball teams. (Fast-pitch softball is explored further in the following chapter.)

Born and raised in St. Paul, Ray "Red" Presley was a three-sport athlete at Mechanic Arts in the late 1940s. An article by Don Riley in the *St. Paul Pioneer Press* on June 24, 1949, praised Presley's basketball talents, calling him a "candidate for the world renowned [Harlem] Globetrotters." Riley also noted that Presley had previously pitched for the Colored House of David baseball team. In a game against Watertown, South Dakota, he reportedly struck out fourteen batters.

Presley received baseball and basketball scholarships to A&T College in Greensboro, North Carolina, but according to the *St. Paul Recorder* of August 23, 1979, "Jim Crow laws forced him to leave after a short stay." He attended the University of Minnesota in 1950 and played freshman basketball until "the high price of education caught up to him and he had to leave." He next joined the air force and there, too, played basketball and baseball. Presley eventually earned a bachelor's degree in political science with a criminal justice studies minor. At the time of the 1979 article, he served as an inspector with the Minneapolis Police Department and was the highest-ranking African American on the force.

Presley is a real success story from St. Paul, an athlete who survived the indignities of Jim Crow, not only in Minnesota but in North Carolina as well. I always looked up to "Red," who played sports at Mechanic Arts with my uncle Eugene "Rock" White.

Over in Minneapolis, LeRoy Hardeman was a star baseball and basketball player at South High School. In Hardeman's obituary, Bud Grant, Hall of Fame coach of the Minnesota Vikings, gave him high accolades, calling him "probably the most outstanding amateur athlete of his era."

I was able to watch and play alongside LeRoy for several years in fast-pitch softball. Other teams always respected his hitting abilities. Hardeman played third base for most of his career and later did a little pitching. He and my father were inducted into the Minnesota Sports Federation's Softball Hall of Fame in 1986 for their outstanding careers.

Many other great black athletes starred at Twin Cities high schools and tore up the rec leagues during the 1940s. In St. Paul, Welcome Hall field was ground zero for seeing the best black players of the day. According to Norm "Speed" Rawlings, who worked at Garrett's pool hall across the street, "people lined up all around Welcome Hall field" to watch games between the all-black clubs. When the great Babe Price would show up—late, invariably—the announcement would be made, "Here comes the Babe!" His was always the grand entrance.

Jim Robinson, a regular at Welcome Hall field back in those days, recalls that "Big" Charlie Anderson was one of the top pitchers around. There is very little documentation about him, however. In the game between the Twin City Colored Giants and the Wakanda Braves in Menomonie discussed earlier, Anderson was listed as the starting pitcher but was scratched for some reason.

Ken Christian, a left-handed hitter, played all positions in the field. He had an amazing technique for drag bunts, holding the bat with his left hand and starting to run toward first while still in the batter's box, somehow making contact with the pitch. By the time an infielder picked up the bunted ball, Kenny would be safely past first base. He once tried out for the Kansas City Monarchs but didn't make the team.

Chinx Worley was an outfielder with a great arm. When a ball was hit in the air to him with runners on base, Chinx was known to yell out "Tag 'em" as he waited for the ball to get to him, showing the confidence he had in his ability to throw runners out.

St. Paul's own Cecil Littles, a third baseman, was with the Bartlesville (Oklahoma) Blues in early 1951 when George White encouraged him to go play with the Estevan Maple Leafs in the Western Canada League. According to Cecil's wife, Mary, she moved back to Oklahoma while Cecil played ball in Canada, but "it was too difficult to have two households on a baseball salary." The couple returned to St. Paul to continue with their lives there, and Cecil played locally with the Colored Giants and then the Ted Bies Liquors fast-pitch softball team. Cecil had tremendous reflexes, and it was hard to get one past him at third. On many occasions when a "smoker" came to him, he would drop to his knees and throw the runner out from that position, making it all look easy.

Jake "Rocking Chair" Foots was a catcher who could catch and throw to second base while sitting in a rocking chair. One of the great stories about Foots is from John Cotton via Norm Rawlings. "The guys were playing at Dunning Field," Rawlings recalled, "and Jake hit a long fly ball just as the streetcar was making its turn just north of the field, on Rondo Avenue. The ball bounced and landed on top of the streetcar, and the centerfielder continued to run down the ball. It dropped off the streetcar roof, and the centerfielder picked it up and threw to the cutoff shortstop, who in turn threw Jake out at third base. For anyone else, this hit would have been a home run, but for Jake 'Slow of Foot' Foots—well, maybe he should have stayed at second."

Among the other players whose names come up in discussions of black baseball in the Twin Cities in the 1940s are the following: Horace Brown, Larry "Bubba" Brown, Peter Buford, Leon Combs, Jack Cooper, Albert Cotton, Buda Crowe, Hiram "Ham" Douglas, Lloyd Gamble, Lloyd "DuLov" Hogan, Norman "Rock Bottom" Howell, Johnny Kelly, Jimmy Lee, Clarence Lewis, Leo Lewis, Jake Lynch, Sam Lynch, Vic McGowan, W. D. Massey, Paul Michaels, Leon Presley, Drexel Pugh, Joe Ray, Paul Ray, Dick Smith Jr., Martin Weddington, Lloyd Wendel, and Sid Williams.

Although the Twin Cities was a breeding ground for this rich pool of talented ballplayers, and even though Jackie Robinson, Larry Doby, and others had broken down the barriers for African Americans in the highest levels of the sport, baseball was beginning to lose the "sport of choice" label for many young black athletes in Minnesota. They were increasingly turning their attention elsewhere, to sports like track, basketball, and football, particularly beginning in high school. These sports appeared to offer greater opportunities at the collegiate level, and scholarships to play these sports at all-black colleges and universities provided a chance to get an education and, hopefully, land a job after college.

Kids from the Twin Cities African American communities did continue to play baseball at the youth level, such as for the Hallie Q. Brown midget squad, which won the city midget championship in 1942 and '43. Dennis Ware and George White's local teams also continued to attract players because of the respect those two all-black teams held in the community, and it was an opportunity to compete at a high level. But at the high school level and beyond, young black athletes were moving away from baseball and onto other sports by the end of the 1940s and into the 1950s.

Black Baseball Rosters of the 1940s

1940 COLLINS & GARRICK, ST. PAUL
From April 12 edition
of Minneapolis Spokesman

Dennis Ware (manager)
Jake Foots (c)

1940 KITTEN BALL (SOFTBALL)
From May 3 edition
of Minneapolis Spokesman

Earl Cannon (manager)
Pete Buford (3B)
George Cummings (CF)
Tommy English (utility)
Littleton Gardner (1B)
Al Harris (C)
Andrew Hartshorn (RSS)
Bobby Jones (LF)
Cleveland Ray (RF)
Manley Rhodes (utility)
Simmie Scroggins (P)

Otis Skinner (RSS)
Stanley Tabor (LSS)
Don Taylor (C)
James Toliver (P)
Lawrence Wycoff (2B)

1942 COLLINS & GARRICK BASEBALL TEAM, ST. PAUL
From May 8 edition of Minneapolis Spokesman

Dennis Ware (manager)
Breedlove (OF)
Cotton (SS)
Jake Foots (C)
Lloyd Gambol (3B)
Percy Hughes (3B)
Jones (OF)
Rosby (2B)
Stone (OF)
Stanly Tabor (1B)
Worley (OF)

1942 MINNEAPOLIS–ST. PAUL GOPHERS
From Todd Peterson, Early Black Baseball in Minnesota *(McFarland & Co, 2010)*

Jim Brown (manager)
Boering (P)
Johnny Britton (3B)
"Lefty" Brown (P)
F. Burns (P/LF)
J. Burns (1B/LF)
Cook (RF)
Davis (P/2B)
Ulysses "Cowboy" Evans (P)
Vic Galloway (P)
Prim "Babe" Hall (1B/P)
Rufus Hatten (C)
Joe "Barney" Higdon (P/RF)
"Big" Jim Johnson (P)
Leamon Johnson (3B)
Collins Jones (SS)
Mack (2B)
Matthews (P)
Gready "Lefty" McKinnis (P)
George Perisee (LF)
Ted "Double Duty" Radcliffe (C/P)
Samuel Seagraves (RF/LF/CF)
Simpson (2B)
Reese "Goose" Tatum (LF/1B)
Thomas (3B/2B)
"Copperknee" Thompson (2B/SS)
Oscar "Bish" Tyson (CF)
Art Wilbert (LF)

1944 TWIN CITY COLORED GIANTS, ST. PAUL

From Todd Peterson, Early Black Baseball in Minnesota *(McFarland & Co, 2010)*

George White (manager/LF)
Phil Archer (P)
Maceo Breedlove (P)
Foots (C)
A. Guiden (RF)
G. Haskins (CF)
James (C)
Johnson (SS)
Jones (CF)
A. Jones (LF)
J. Jones (C)
Preston (SS)
Reddick (SS/3B)
L. Smith (2B/1B)
E. Tinsley (RF/utility)
Warberg (2B)
Louis "Pud" White (3B/P)
Chinx Worley (2B)

1947 TWIN CITY COLORED GIANTS, ST. PAUL

From June 25 scorebook, Twin City Colored Giants vs. Wakanda Braves, Menomonie, Wisconsin

Howell (CF)
Presley (2B)
Cotton (3B)
Bankhead (C)
P. White (SS)
Price (P)
G. White (LF)
Smith (RF)
Anderson (P)
Oler (1B)

Youth Teams

●◦●◦●◦●◦●

1940 HALLIE Q. BROWN MIDGETS

Dwight Reed (coach)
Frank Brown (OF)
Boyd Collins (OF)
Milton Combs (OF)
Sterling Duke (OF)
Kimeal Ellis (3B)
Sherman Harper (OF)
Hugh Schuck (P)
George Washington (1B)
Louis "Pud" White (C)
Raymond "Red" Presley (bat boy)

1943 HALLIE Q. BROWN MIDGETS

Walter Archer (P)
Clyde Carson (C)
Roland Carson (1B)
Horace Collins (RF)
Jack Kinney (3B)
Ted McDade (LF)
Red Presley (SS)
Dick Smith Jr. (3B)
Kermit Wheeler (CF)

·6·
The 1950s

The Decline of Black Baseball
and the Rise of Fast-Pitch Softball

THE 1950S WAS A TUMULTUOUS DECADE for race relations in the United States, and baseball provided a temporary distraction from the continuing challenges of everyday life for Minnesota's black population. On January 25, 1952, a front-page headline in the *Minneapolis Spokesman* read, "Minnesota Still Has Racial Problem, Says Governor's Commission—Racial problem areas, relatively untouched, still remain in Minnesota."

While Governor Elmer Anderson and his Interracial Commission studied the problems of race in Minnesota, Thurgood Marshall and others were spearheading the legal challenges to segregated schools on the national front with the landmark *Brown v. Board of Education* case, which went all the way to the Supreme Court. The unanimous decision delivered by Chief Justice Earl Warren on May 14, 1954, proclaimed that "in the field of public education the doctrine of 'separate but equal' has no place. Separate educational facilities are inherently unequal." It was a milestone moment that would accelerate the process of desegregation, particularly in the South. But even with this acceleration, there was still a long way to go.

The end of segregation in organized baseball the previous decade had many African American baseball fans energized heading into the 1950s, in the Twin Cities and elsewhere. Black fans were attending games at St. Paul's Lexington Park and Minneapolis's Nicollet Park to watch superstars like Roy Campanella, Dan Bankhead, Jim Pendleton, Dave Barnhill,

Picketers outside Woolworth's in St. Paul protesting the chain's segregated lunch counters.
Minnesota Historical Society Collections

and Ray Dandridge suit up for the American Association's Saints and Millers, some of them on their way to the major leagues.

The biggest name to land in Minnesota at this time didn't stick around for very long, but he tore up the American Association during his brief stay in Minneapolis. On July 28, 1950, a *Spokesman* headline announced, "Millers Purchase 19 Year Old Outfielder Willie Mays." The article praised Mays as a "promising Negro youngster who may eclipse the fame of other members of his race now playing in the Major Leagues." The investment by the New York Giants, the Millers' parent club, was "greater than any sum paid" for Jackie Robinson, Roy Campanella, Don Newcombe, or Larry

Doby. The Giants not only compensated the Birmingham Black Barons, Mays's Negro League team, but also gave the young outfielder a "substantial bonus," according to the *Spokesman*.

In only thirty-five games with the Millers in 1951, Mays tallied a .477 batting average, 8 homers, and 30 runs batted in. He made his debut with the New York Giants on May 25—and the rest is history.

Another Minnesota stomping ground for up-and-coming talent during the 1950s was St. Cloud, where the Rox of the Northern League served as the C-level affiliate for the Giants. Several future major leaguers spent time in St. Cloud during the 1950s, as well as after the Rox became a farm team for the Chicago Cubs in 1960.

Prior to the 1953 season, the Giants organization signed the twenty-one-year-old Dominican-born Ozzie Virgil as an amateur free agent. His first stop in pro ball was with the St. Cloud Rox. He worked his way up to the Triple-A Minneapolis Millers, for whom he played third base in 1956. He got the call up to the Giants that September and became the first player from the Dominican Republic in the major leagues.

Willie Mays of the Minneapolis Millers, 1951. Minnesota Historical Society Collections

One of Ozzie's teammates with the Rox in 1953 was John Kennedy, who in 1957 would become the first African American to play for the Philadelphia Phillies. Kennedy's major league career lasted only five games and two at bats, but he remained in organized ball through the end of the decade.

The season after Virgil and Kennedy, St. Cloud boasted another future major leaguer on its Rox roster. Willie Kirkland was the Northern League's top hitter in 1954 with a .360 average for St. Cloud. From there, Kirkland made his way through Class B and C before landing in Minneapolis to play for the Millers in late 1955 and then a full season in 1956. His major league debut with the San Francisco Giants came on April 15, 1958; he batted cleanup in the franchise's first game on the West Coast. On either side of Kirkland in the Giants' lineup that day were two other black stars who had spent time in Minneapolis: Willie Mays and Orlando Cepeda.

Ozzie Virgil

ABOUT TEN YEARS AGO, at the Minnesota Amateur Baseball Hall of Fame, located in the St. Cloud convention center, I noticed a display celebrating St. Cloud's black baseball history. On view were photos of such stars as Lou Brock, Orlando Cepeda, Willie Kirkland, Ozzie Virgil Sr., and others wearing the uniform of the St. Cloud Rox. Here was evidence of St. Cloud's important legacy in Minnesota black baseball.

In 2014, while working on this book, I had the pleasure and privilege of interviewing Ozzie Virgil Sr. about his career. I was connected to him through Alejandro De Moya and Osiris Ramirez, both of whom work for the office of the commissioner of Major League Baseball in the Dominican Republic and whom I met at an event for the MLB-RBI Institute.

Virgil was born in the Dominican Republic and later immigrated with his family to New York and went to high school in the Bronx. When he made his debut with the New York Giants on September 23, 1956, he was the first major league baseball player from the Dominican Republic—a nation that has since produced hundreds and hundreds of major leaguers.

Two years later, Virgil was traded to the Detroit Tigers and made history again by becoming the first black player to suit up for one of the last teams to break the color barrier.

When I was a young kid and boasted a great baseball card collection, included in my holdings was an Ozzie Virgil card. Not only did Ozzie have a major league career that lasted more than a decade, but he played here in Minnesota. To interview one of the players who broke the color line for a major league team was a particular honor for me.

Virgil had positive recollections of his time in St. Cloud, saying that it was a nice city and that people treated him well. He didn't make much money in Class C baseball, but he enjoyed playing for Charlie Fox, who later managed the Giants.

While with the Minneapolis Millers in 1956, Virgil played for manager Eddie Stanky, a former major league player and manager. He said that Stanky was a tough guy, but he learned a lot from him. In fact, he learned a lot about the game of baseball at this level.

The Millers had just moved into the new Metropoli-

Cepeda's rise through the minors was even quicker than Kirkland's. He starred for the St. Cloud Rox in 1956, topping the Northern League with 26 homers and a .355 average. He was promoted to the Triple-A Millers in 1957, where he batted .309 with 25 homers and 108 runs batted in. By opening day 1958, the Puerto Rico native was the starting first baseman for the San Francisco Giants. He homered in the game and went on to be named the National League's Rookie of the Year.

The 1955 Rox featured three black players who would later enjoy major league careers. Andre Rodgers, Tony Taylor, and Leon Wagner helped St. Cloud to a 78–47 record in the Northern League that year. Wagner, who went on to hit more than 200 home runs at the major league level, led the circuit with 29 homers; Rodgers was second with 28 while leading all Northern Leaguers with a .387 average. Rodgers, who also played with Cepeda in Minneapolis in 1957, was originally from the Bahamas. Taylor,

tan Stadium in Bloomington, where there wasn't a lot of housing available, mostly just farmland. Virgil explained that the players had to live in a hotel/motel; he recalled that it was nice and people "were great to us."

Because of the open space surrounding the stadium, Virgil says that swirling winds made it hard to hit to leftfield. During that season with the Millers, he played alongside several black players who later reached the major leagues: Willie Kirkland, Bill Taylor, Valmy Thomas, and Bill White. He also recalls playing against Lacey Curry and Solly Drake, stars of the rival St. Paul Saints.

Virgil was called up to the New York Giants in September 1956 and appeared in the final three games of the season. He played in 96 games for the Giants in 1957 and then was traded to Detroit on January 28, 1958.

Becoming the first black player to play for the Detroit Tigers was an exciting moment for him. He shared with a chuckle his recollection that, when he arrived in Detroit, some of the city's African American fans were disappointed because he was Domini-

can and not African American. They soon became supportive of Virgil, however, during his time with the team from 1958 to 1961.

Over the rest of the decade, Virgil would bounce around to the Kansas City Athletics, Baltimore Orioles, and Pittsburgh Pirates before landing back with the franchise where he got his start, although now on the other side of the country as the San Francisco Giants, following the 1965 season. He remained with the organization, playing mostly in Triple-A, until manager Clyde King offered him a coaching job with the big league club in 1969. Thus began a coaching career in the major leagues that lasted twenty years.

Ozzie is very proud of his history in the game. "I'm honored to have played the great game of baseball at the highest level," he said. To this day, in his eighties, he misses the sound of the bat and tries to stay involved with the sport. In February 2014, Virgil was inducted into the Latino Baseball Hall of Fame, located in his homeland of the Dominican Republic. (His son, Ozzie Virgil Jr., played in the major leagues from 1980 to 1990.) ●

Former St. Cloud Rox players Willie Kirkland, Orlando Cepeda, and Ozzie Virgil, 1956. Myron Hall Collection, Stearns History Museum, St. Cloud, Minnesota

a Cuba native, was just nineteen when he joined the Rox in '55; he was the everyday second baseman for the Chicago Cubs by the time he was twenty-two. Taylor played a total of nineteen seasons in the majors, including fifteen with the Philadelphia Phillies.

The Giants organization continued to scout Latin America and the Caribbean for baseball talent, and in the late 1950s they signed three brothers from the Dominican Republic: Felipe, Matty, and Jesus Alou. The oldest, Felipe, played briefly with the Millers in 1957 and ascended to the majors in '58. Jesus, the youngest of the three, was signed by the Giants when he was just seventeen years old in 1959. He bypassed Minnesota but made his way to the big leagues in 1963. The middle brother, Matty, played Class C

Current and former Minneapolis Millers players at an exhibition game between the Millers and New York Giants, 1957. From left to right: Pete Burnside, Ozzie Virgil Sr., Orlando Cepeda, Willie Kirkland, and Ray Katt. Stearns History Museum, St. Cloud, Minnesota

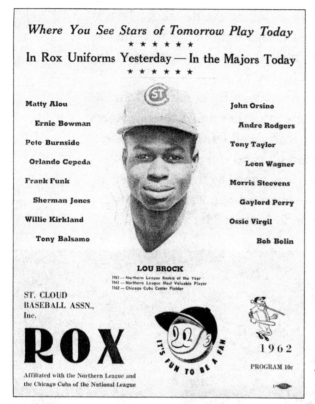

Where You See Stars of Tomorrow Play Today
★ ★ ★ ★ ★ ★
In Rox Uniforms Yesterday — In the Majors Today
★ ★ ★ ★ ★ ★

Matty Alou

Ernie Bowman

Pete Burnside

Orlando Cepeda

Frank Funk

Sherman Jones

Willie Kirkland

Tony Balsamo

John Orsino

Andre Rodgers

Tony Taylor

Leon Wagner

Morris Steevens

Gaylord Perry

Ossie Virgil

Bob Bolin

LOU BROCK
1961 — Northern League Rookie of the Year
1961 — Northern League Most Valuable Player
1962 — Chicago Cubs Center Fielder

ST. CLOUD
BASEBALL ASSN.,
Inc.

ROX
IT'S FUN TO BE A FAN

1962
PROGRAM 10c

Affiliated with the Northern League and
the Chicago Cubs of the National League

St. Cloud Rox program cover, featuring former Rox Lou Brock, 1962

ball with the St. Cloud Rox in 1958 and posted a .321 average that year. His major league debut came in 1960. The three brothers would play alongside one another in the San Francisco Giants outfield during the 1963 season.

After fourteen years as a Giants affiliate, the St. Cloud Rox became part of the Chicago Cubs' farm system beginning in 1960. The following year, the team hosted another future Hall of Famer. In 1961, St. Cloud's Lou Brock led the Northern League with a .361 average, 117 runs, and 38 stolen bases. It was his one and only minor league season before joining the Cubs that September.

Future Hall of Famers weren't the only ones making headlines in the local sports press during this time. Dick Smith, a graduate of St. Paul's Marshall Senior High School, signed a deal with the Giants just a few weeks before Mays did in July 1950. As Jimmy Griffin reported in his "Saintly City Sports" column in the *Spokesman*, "Dick Smith, 20 year old youngster, was signed by the New York Giants last week and assigned to Davenport, Iowa in the Three Eye League. He is the son of Richard Smith, 767 St. Anthony Ave., and has been quite an all-around athlete. He played hockey and football with Marshall High and was Golden Gloves lightweight champ. He carries with him the best wishes of the local citizens. We hope he will make the grade in Davenport and someday with the Giants." Unfortunately, Smith never did play with the Giants.

Fellow Marshall athlete Leo Lewis was on all-city teams in football, basketball, and track in high school. He went on to play football at Lincoln University and then played professionally in Canada, spending eleven seasons with the Winnipeg Blue Bombers of the Canadian Football League. Lewis was inducted into both the College Football Hall of Fame and the Canadian Football Hall of Fame. During the summer of 1950, however, before his first year at Lincoln, Lewis played baseball for George White and the Twin City Colored Giants. He was a pitcher and also had some home run power at the plate.

The Colored Giants continued to barnstorm throughout the Midwest and Canada during the first half of the 1950s. "The Twin City Giants won a doubleheader 5–3 and 2–1 at White Bear Lake July 4 and came back on July 10th to defeat the St. Paul All Nations team 7–6 at New Richmond, Wis.," reported Griffin on July 15, 1955.

Barnstorming

THE CHALLENGES AND DANGERS involved in traveling as a black barnstorming team—whether for baseball or basketball—continued for many years, even in the North. I remember a trip I took with my father's basketball team, the Clippers, when I was about sixteen years old. This team included some former pro and college players as well as standout locals like my father. I had finished my junior year on the Mechanic Arts High School varsity team and was invited along, as a sixth man, for a weekend basketball trip to northern Wisconsin.

We arrived in the first town after the long drive from the Twin Cities. The gym was in great need of repair, colder inside than out, and the pipes had frozen so we couldn't take showers after the game. But the real shock to me was when it came time to find a place to eat. We stopped at a local bar and restaurant, and as the other players stayed outside to chat with some folks who had been at the game, I went in. Right inside the entrance, I noticed a handmade poster that read, "Come and see the St. Paul Nigger Clowns play basketball." It had the date, time, and location of our game and included a very demeaning caricature of an African American basketball player. I immediately went out and told my father that we couldn't eat there.

"Why not?" he asked. I led him and the others into the place and pointed to the poster. My dad and the four other players all laughed. I didn't see the humor in it; I was shocked that such a poster would be allowed in public.

The following day, we traveled to the next town, in a small resort area, for the second game. When we arrived, we stopped at a small café tucked into a stand of birch trees. As we got out of the car, I looked at the front door and saw the blinds being pulled shut; a hand reached out to turn the sign from "Open" to "Closed." I continued up the walkway only to find the door locked. Just then a patrol car pulled up, and the officer asked, "Are you guys the basketball team?" My father told him we were, and the officer asked us to follow him. Once again, the others laughed while I failed to see what was so funny. The officer took us around the lake to another location where we were permitted to eat.

All these years later, I understand that the players' laughter was really a recognition that this turn of events was nothing new to them. They knew that if they fought the injustice, they likely wouldn't be asked to return for more games—and a chance to earn some extra money. ●

Odell Livingston and Fred Ackers. Courtesy of Lorna Livingston Pettis

But an era in Minnesota baseball was coming to an end. The Twin City Colored Giants—the area's last all-black team—were playing their final season in 1955. Black teams had been gradually losing the attention and passion of fans and the African American press, who were focusing more on the integrated Saints and Millers teams and on the growing number of black players in the major league ranks.

Following Gread McKinnis's breakthrough with Rochester in the 1947 state tournament, more semipro and town ball clubs were opening their rosters to African Americans. The Delano Athletic Club of the North Star League had two black players in 1950: Odell Livingston, a switch-hitting catcher, and Fred Ackers, a pitcher and part-time outfielder. Clippings from the *Delano Eagle*—provided by Livingston's daughter, Lorna Livingston Pettis of North Minneapolis—reveal that Livingston and Ackers also played for the Colored House of David team prior to joining Delano.

In the Southern Minnesota League, Dick Newberry was a star second baseman for the Wasetonna Twins (a merging of teams from Waseca and Owatonna) in 1956. A notice in the *Spokesman* announced that Newberry was to be honored before a game against Austin on July 15: "The only colored ball player in Southern Minnesota, . . . Newberry has led the entire league in hitting and currently sports a .416 average, which includes 37 hits in 89 times at bat. He has nine doubles, a triple and three home runs to his credit." Called the sharpest second baseman in the Southern Minny, Newberry had been with the Duluth Dukes of the Northern League before joining Wasetonna.

The integration of baseball—whether the Brooklyn Dodgers and New York Giants or the St. Paul Saints and Minneapolis Millers or the Delano Athletic Club and Wasetonna Twins—brought enthusiasm and a sense of hope to the black communities of Minnesota, and the excitement of going to the ballpark to cheer for these new stars was a positive development. But baseball was at a turning point among African American athletes in Minnesota, and it seemed to be turning in the wrong direction.

For several years in his column for the *Spokesman*, Jimmy Griffin expressed frustration with the absence of young blacks on area high school baseball teams. "The St. Paul baseball nines are in action starting the 1954 season," he wrote on April 16 of that year. "Conspicuous by their absence are Negro players. As this columnist has pointed out before, here is a field which has been thrown wide open and we don't have the participation by our Negro lads that we should have. St. Paul high school baseball is without a doubt the strongest in the state and we should encourage our Saintly City boys to try out for baseball. There is a great future in this sport in money and fame."

Just as semipro clubs like the Twin City Colored Giants were having trouble staying afloat due to waning interest, the athletes that had played baseball as younger kids were turning their attention to other sports as they entered high school. Even with the dismantling of the color line, both at the major league level and among town and semipro teams, openings in baseball remained limited for African Americans. Multisport athletes looked increasingly to football and basketball, where opportunities were more prevalent at traditional black colleges as well as at local colleges and universities. The sports culture was shifting that way, and word of mouth in the community challenged the dream that a professional baseball career was a viable option. As the older guys talked around the neighborhood, the younger guys learned that the integration of the major leagues in the previous decade had not, in fact, introduced that many opportunities for black players. After all, how many local guys had made it? How many were playing in local colleges?

One activity to which some adults began to turn for fun and competition around this time was fast-pitch softball. The sport took Minnesota by storm in the 1950s. Players who used to play baseball looked to fast-pitch softball, which required many of the same skills as baseball. The different style of pitching, however, created a new challenge, as batters had to learn how to hit a ball traveling 90 miles an hour but coming up as opposed to going down.

The Amateur Softball Association (ASA) created a system of regional and national tournaments attracting the top teams in the country, similar to the model in amateur and semipro baseball. The Twin Cities would dominate the highest level of fast-pitch softball for decades. Among the top class was the Belmont team from St. Paul, which later became the Whitaker Buick team and then the All American Bar team, its core always featuring some of the best fast-pitch players in the country. Another important item to note about this team—similar to the situation in town baseball—is that several players, especially pitchers, were paid.

Beginning in the early 1950s, references to the Ted Bies Liquor fast-pitch softball team featured regularly in the local African American press. In his *Spokesman* column, Griffin described games between Ted Bies and such teams as the 216th AROTC and Conroy and Farr. The June 19, 1953, edition noted, "Ted Bies won again Friday, June 12, in the Midway Open softball league, 5–3. Simmy Scroggins and Lou White were the winning battery." A year later: "Ted Bies trounced Phyllis Wheatley 11–4 in a softball game, Sunday, June 20, at Sumner Field in Minneapolis." Scroggins and White made up the winning battery again in a 14–1 victory over the Stahl House in a Midway Open softball game reported in July 1955. And on August 10, 1956, the *Spokesman* carried the following story:

Ted Bies Snaps New Bar's Winning Streak

Bies scored its first run in the opening inning on Lou White's single that drove in the singling Ken Christian, and added five in the third to chase starter Emery Tako from the mound. Bies batted around in the big inning with Christian's single and White's double accounting for three runs.

These examples represent just a small sampling to illustrate the growing presence of fast-pitch softball. Guys who had played baseball were now turning to softball, in the Twin Cities and throughout Minnesota. The old rivalries among St. Paul teams and between the cities were transferred to the softball field.

Ted Bies Liquor Store fast-pitch softball team

St. Paul produced some of the best fast-pitch teams in Minnesota, with many advancing to ASA regional and national tournaments. My father, Lou "Pud" White, later made the move to the Minneapolis Classic League, which played at Parade Stadium near the intersection of Lyndale Avenue and Dunwoody Boulevard. Although his reasons for switching to Minneapolis are not entirely clear, he did receive some stipends to play.

My father thrived in the Minneapolis Classic League, as he had throughout his career as a hitter and defensive catcher. He would win three batting titles, with a batting average over .300 for each. He not only hit for average but could take pitchers out of the park with long drives. When he was behind the plate as a catcher, no one stole second base on Lou White; he had a great arm. In baseball, you steal on the pitcher; in fast-pitch softball, you steal on the catcher.

In 1986, my father was inducted into the Minnesota Sports Federation's Softball Hall of Fame along with his good friend and teammate on the Minneapolis side, LeRoy Hardeman.

As the 1950s came to a close, the situation in Minnesota black baseball was far different than it had been a decade earlier. Where men like Jimmy Griffin, Harry Davis, and Jimmy Lee—all former ballplayers themselves—had once provided an important service to the community by shedding light on Minnesota's black athletes in the African American press, sports coverage was shifting away from the local scene and more to those who had been signed into organized baseball. This accelerated the demise of the Negro Leagues and of barnstorming black teams, as fans became focused on the black players who had "made it." With less attention paid to the local baseball action, young African Americans were increasingly turning their attention to other sports.

Oxford Giants baseball team, with coach Bob "Big Six" Carter, 1958

My Memories of Rondo

IN 1955, MY FAMILY MOVED to 409 St. Anthony Avenue, into a duplex owned by one of my father's good friends, Frank Brown, who lived next door at 407 St. Anthony. The home was located a half block from the Ober Boys Club field, previously known as Welcome Hall field and the field that my father had played on many times with the Twin City Colored Giants, although I did not learn this detail until much later.

In the opening of this book I shared my cherished memories of playing catch with my father when we lived at this house, and I have many other fond recollections of these days living in the Rondo neighborhood. Another favorite moment with my father was when he would take me down to the pool hall owned by Othello Walker at the corner of Western and St. Anthony Avenues, the old bar that had sponsored the Collins-Garrick baseball team back in the 1930s and '40s. I would enjoy a chili dog while he had a bowl of chili and, most likely, a beer. Those chili dogs were the best around. Anytime I earned twenty-five cents,

I was off to Mr. Walker's for a chili dog. Mr. Walker and most of my father's friends would call me "little Lou" or "little Pud."

Another fine gathering place to learn about the world was Wazzie's Barber Shop. (The barber's real name was Clarence Lewis, and his name appears on the roster of the Ted Bies softball team that my father played on as well.) Beginning in 1956, when I was old enough to go to Wazzie's with my father, I loved whenever we could afford to get me a haircut there. My father and others would always get a shave, and I would sit and watch, amazed—and a little scared. Wazzie loved to tell stories, and he would hold that straight razor while gesturing wildly with his hands. I can recall the hot towels and the smell of the aftershave lotion that he would put on my father; sometimes I would even get some splashed on me after a haircut and that straight razor line around my ears. It made me feel so grown up.

continued next page

My Memories of Rondo

continued from previous page

Going to Wazzie's also meant hearing "the men stories"—stories about what was going on in the Rondo neighborhood and lots of sports tales. Of course, some stories were supposed to be for grown-up ears only, but I would listen and act like I didn't know what they were talking about. Later, I was repeating those stories to my friends—all a part of growing up.

I've come to understand that the importance of the weekly visits to the barbershop was about more than just the socializing. It was where the guys would talk and share the latest news from the community or around the country. Most people couldn't afford a TV, and radio news didn't attract a lot of African American listeners, so word of mouth was a vital mode of communication during this time.

Occasionally, some guy would come into the shop and say something to Wazzie, who would interrupt the shave or haircut and go into the back room with him. They'd be away for a short while, and then they'd come out and continue with whatever they had been doing. I later found out that there was always a bottle of some type of liquor in the back room for a little sip and conversation. Ah, the barbershop, the men's gathering place!

Thinking back on our family's move to St. Anthony Avenue, I realize it was a huge change in my life. Before, when we lived on North Dale Street, we were the only family of color in the area. I went to Como Park Elementary School, and although I had good friends that accepted me as one of their buddies, I stood out because of my race.

After we moved to Rondo, our world became mostly African American, and the neighborhood was a safe haven of sorts. To me, it seemed as if St. Paul had a large black population, but I later realized that it was only the case in our immediate community. My sisters and I attended St. Peter Claver Catholic School on St. Anthony Avenue, and the number of students of color there was a dramatic difference from our previous school.

Everything we needed, it seemed, was contained within the boundaries of Rondo: school, church, the grocery store, open lots where we played sports, the Ober Boys Club, and so on. It also contained all my friends, my sports, the elders I respected. People in Rondo were very friendly, and so many people knew my father; I always felt comfortable and safe.

Hollow Playground, over at Kent and St. Anthony, was another favorite place for us kids. It was kind of a dump, with no turf to speak of, but it was one of the few open spaces in Rondo for pickup games in summer. In winter, it was the place where we went ice skating. The Elks Drum and Bugle Corps also practiced at the Hollow, and they would march up and down St. Anthony prior to parades or other celebrations. Everyone would come out of their homes to hear them play—watching, listening to the rhythm and beats, bouncing and dancing on the side of the street as the Elks passed by.

Shortly after we moved to the neighborhood, I began to play pee wee and midget baseball down the street at the Ober Boys Club. The field was bordered by Western Avenue on the west, St. Anthony Avenue to the north (running between the field and the Ober Boys Club building), Virginia Street on the east, and Rondo Avenue on the south. The field was a large rectangular area, with home plate located near the corner of Western and St. Anthony, which put rightfield a short distance away and leftfield a full block away—a long distance for pee wee and midget ballplayers.

Whenever we played a game at home at Ober, the guys across the street at the pool hall would gradually make their way over to the field to watch and talk about the game. I can remember the men saying things from behind the fence like, "Did you see that boy throw the ball?" I had a strong arm for my age—I could throw hard but didn't have much control; in fact, you could say that I was kind of wild—so the coach made me pitch. I would much rather have played shortstop, the position everyone wanted, but it was great to hear these guys from the neighborhood saying positive things about me and my pitching. I enjoyed playing baseball every day, especially when the adults came over to watch and admire us in action.

Our team at Ober was mixed, and I played alongside Roger Neal and William "Wells" Price, among others. Our main rival was the team from Oxford Playground, coached by Bob "Big Six" Carter. A couple of years later, Carter recruited some of us to play on his team, the Giants, in the Oxford house league, which included several all-black teams. Whenever we played at Oxford, it seemed that the sport of baseball was alive and well in the black community of the Twin Cities, but in the cities at large, the number was small.

No dreams of playing in the major leagues, no concerns about the color barrier—we just played because we loved the game.

·7·
The 1960s
The End of an Era

THE DECADE OF THE 1960S saw some of the most important civil rights legislation passed since Reconstruction following the Civil War. The Civil Rights Movement had grown and expanded from the local-oriented activism of the 1950s, its leaders now pushing for change at the federal level. The emergence of more radical voices advocating Black Power further altered the dynamics of and the dialogue surrounding race relations across the United States.

At the dawn of the decade, the Civil Rights Act of 1960 was signed into law by President Dwight Eisenhower. It sought to bolster the Civil Rights Act of 1957 in protecting the voting rights of African Americans and bringing stronger enforcement capabilities to the federal courts and the Civil Rights Commission. The Civil Rights Act of 1964, enacted under President Lyndon Johnson, was a landmark piece of legislation that outlawed discrimination in the areas of public accommodations, facilities, and schools on the grounds of race, color, religion, or national origin. Among other provisions, the act also prohibited discrimination in employment and created the Equal Employment Opportunity Commission to enforce it.

Although the 1964 act did include additional clauses intended to protect and ensure voting rights for African Americans, the Voting Rights Act of 1965 went further still to counteract the continuing disenfranchisement of blacks, especially in the South, and to reinforce the rights guaranteed by the Fifteenth Amendment to the U.S. Constitution. The act was introduced to Congress less than two weeks after the violent repression of the civil rights march from Selma to Montgomery, Alabama, on March 7, 1965, also known as "Bloody Sunday."

In addition to providing a spark for the passage of the Voting Rights Act, the Selma march underscores the violence that hung over the movement during the sixties. The following are just a few of the most memorable tragedies and acts of violence.

- June 12, 1963: Medgar Evers, civil rights activist and NAACP leader, is assassinated outside his home in Jackson, Mississippi.
- September 15, 1963: Four young girls are killed and twenty-two others are injured in a bombing of the Sixteenth Street Baptist Church in Birmingham, Alabama, by members of the Ku Klux Klan.
- February 21, 1965: Malcolm X is assassinated while giving a speech at the Audubon Ballroom in New York City.
- April 4, 1968: Martin Luther King Jr. is assassinated at the Lorraine Motel in Memphis, Tennessee.
- April 1968: Riots and civil disturbances break out in black communities throughout the United States in the wake of the King assassination.

In addition to these—and many other—racially charged incidents, the sixties also saw the assassination of President John F. Kennedy on November 22, 1963, and of his brother, and presidential candidate, Robert F. Kennedy on June 5, 1968. Riots and protests in opposition to the war in Vietnam spread across college campuses and cities throughout the nation.

Even with the advances of the Civil Rights Movement, and even in a state as far north as Minnesota, African Americans continued to face discrimination in virtually every arena, and many blacks in the Twin Cities experienced it on a firsthand basis.

As late as 1964, so-called covenants remained in effect, dictating where African Americans could and could not live in the Twin Cities. When Dr. Leonard Linnell put his home at 2137 Juno Avenue, near St. Catherine University, up for sale, he received a full-price offer from a young African

American named Lonnie Adkins, a successful architect in town. When neighbors heard of this, they offered Linnell more money to not sell the home to Adkins. Linnell went ahead and sold to Adkins, and in fact reduced the selling amount by $500, telling him, "You'll need to build a garage."

Don Geng, a former member of the Attucks Brooks Legion baseball team, happened to be friends with Lonnie Adkins Jr. Geng remembers Lonnie Jr. telling him that people would burn crosses in their front yard when he was growing up.

The violence and rebellion of the era did reach the Twin Cities as well, later in the 1960s, although not quite to the degree that cities such as Detroit, Newark, and Los Angeles experienced. In July 1967, an altercation between police and two black women during the city's Aquatennial Torchlight Parade sparked unrest in North Minneapolis. Over the course

National Guard troops arrive in North Minneapolis during the Plymouth Avenue riots of July 1967. Minnesota Historical Society Collections

of three nights, the area along Plymouth Avenue saw looting, vandalism, rock throwing, and arson, as racial tensions that had been simmering in Minneapolis's main African American neighborhood came to a boil. National Guard troops were called in to restore order. In the end, thirty-six people were arrested, dozens were injured, and numerous businesses were destroyed by fire, many of them never to reopen.

Minnesota was not immune to the campus activism of the period, either. In January 1969, African American students from the Afro-American Action Committee (AAAC) led the takeover of the Morrill Hall administration building on the Minneapolis campus of the University of Minnesota. Among the issues the AAAC wanted addressed by the university were the need for an African American studies department, the lack of scholarships and financial aid for students of color, a shortage of faculty members of color, and discrimination in campus housing. Some seventy students occupied the building for about twenty-four hours until an agreement was reached with university officials.

The climate at Division I schools with regard to black athletes was changing as well, and the University of Minnesota started recruiting more African Americans for its sports teams. Sandy Stephens had been signed in 1958 as the university's first black quarterback. Running back Bill Munsey, fullback Judge Dickson, and lineman Bobby Bell soon followed, and the impact was immediate. The Gophers won a national championship in 1960 and played in back-to-back Rose Bowls following the 1960 and '61 seasons.

In 1963, the university signed three black athletes to basketball scholarships: Lou Hudson, Don Yates, and Archie Clark. All three helped bring success for the Gophers on the hardwood in the middle years of the decade, and all three would be drafted into the National Basketball Association. In 1965, Leroy Gardner Jr. became the first Minnesota-born African American to receive a basketball scholarship at the University of Minnesota.

While the black stars on the local university basketball team generated excitement among African Americans in the Twin Cities, on the national scene the National Collegiate Athletic Association (NCAA) championship won by Texas Western College (now the University of Texas at El Paso) in 1966 truly shook up collegiate sports. The Texas Western Miners featured an all-black starting lineup, and to win the title they defeated the all-white Kentucky Wildcats—a basketball powerhouse coached by Adolph Rupp, who did not sign the university's first African American player until 1969. Texas Western's triumph under a national spotlight served to underscore the segregation that was still evident in college athletics, particularly among southern schools, and it helped to spur the recruitment of black athletes by previously all-white programs.

African Americans were also making a greater impact at the pro level. The Boston Celtics dynasty, which won ten of eleven NBA titles between 1959 and 1969, featured several prominent black players, including Bill Russell, Sam Jones, K. C. Jones, and Tom Sanders. The '66 champion Celtics had a total of seven black players on its twelve-man roster.

Every year from 1958 to 1962, the number-one player selected in the NBA draft was African American—including future Hall of Famers Elgin Baylor, Oscar Robertson, and Walt Bellamy—and five more black players secured the top pick during the 1960s. In the 1967 draft, the first six players selected were all black. Also during this period, players such as Willis Reed of Grambling State University (1964), Bob Love of Southern University and A&M College (1965), and Earl "the Pearl" Monroe of Winston-Salem State University (1967) came out of historic black colleges to great acclaim in the pros.

Between the star black athletes being recruited at major white universities and those making the transition from black schools to the NBA, young African Americans in the Twin Cities and elsewhere began to see brighter prospects in basketball.

By 1963, my final year in high school sports, only three African Americans were playing baseball in the St. Paul high school conference: Art Smith and Bill Reizer at Central High School and me at Mechanic Arts High School. Basketball had become the sport of choice. Beginning in tenth grade, I tried to play basketball every day. Even after baseball practice, I would go off to play basketball, practicing and then practicing some more.

Following the baseball season of my senior year, I received an invitation to attend a baseball camp, but Coach Howie Schultz advised me not to go. I'm not sure why: was it because the opportunities in baseball were so limited, or because I wasn't good enough? (I hope not.) Regardless, it was already clear at this point that basketball was the direction I was pursuing for college—another example of local African American youths turning their attention away from baseball.

By the time I arrived at the University of Minnesota, I was all in with basketball. But earlier in the decade, as young teenagers, my friends and I still loved to play baseball, and we were big fans of the major leagues. I had a baseball card collection that was second to none. I would do errands for neighbors just to earn a little extra money that I could use to buy baseball cards a box at a time. At home, I created my own baseball game and league, using dice and lineups from the newspaper or my baseball cards. I even kept statistics.

Important Moments in Black Baseball of the 1960s

AUGUST 21, 1960: Comiskey Park in Chicago hosts its last East-West All-Star Game. The annual Negro League midsummer classic had been played there nearly every year since 1933.

1962: Buck O'Neil is hired by the Chicago Cubs to become the first black coach in major league baseball.

JULY 23, 1962: Jackie Robinson becomes the first former Negro League player inducted into the National Baseball Hall of Fame at Cooperstown.

AUGUST 27, 1962: The last East-West All-Star Game is played at Municipal Stadium in Kansas City, former home of the Kansas City Monarchs.

AUGUST 1962: The Negro American League officially folds following the East-West All-Star Game. Even though there is no official league, four teams—Indianapolis Clowns, Kansas City Monarchs, Philadelphia Stars, and Satchel Paige All Stars—continue to play a barnstorming schedule. By the end of the decade, only the Indianapolis Clowns remain.

1963: Elston Howard of the New York Yankees becomes the first African American to win the Most Valuable Player Award in the American League.

1964: Willie Mays is named captain of the San Francisco Giants, the first black to be so honored by a major league team.

MARCH 11, 1966: Emmett Ashford becomes the first black umpire in major league baseball, in a spring training game between the Cleveland Indians and the Washington Senators.

My friends and I continued with our pickup games and playing at Ober Boys Club and Oxford playground. I got to play on a team from White Bear after one of my father's softball teammates found out that I was a pitcher. He would take me to the ballpark, which had a green fence all around the field. It was like a mini-stadium.

Even though at the youth level there was still widespread passion for baseball, we knew that the end was near. Many of us played two or three sports, changing with the seasons, and as we got to high school, the best players usually opted for sports other than baseball. By my count, only four African American ballplayers from the Twin Cities pursued baseball at the college level during the 1960s.

Those of us who were entering high school and college around this time had watched our fathers play baseball with the great black teams of the 1940s, when the sport was held in high esteem in the Twin Cities African American communities. But the opportunities to watch adults

AUGUST 1968: Monte Irvin is hired as assistant director of public relations and promotions for the office of the commissioner of Major League Baseball, becoming the first African American to hold an executive position in the league headquarters. He served under William "Spike" Eckert and Bowie Kuhn for a total of sixteen years.

OCTOBER 22, 1968: Elston Howard is hired by the Yankees to be their first-base coach, becoming the first black coach for an American League team.

JULY 28, 1969: Roy Campanella becomes the second African American inducted into the Hall of Fame.

DECEMBER 24, 1969: St. Louis Cardinals outfielder Curt Flood writes to commissioner Bowie Kuhn asserting his right to become a free agent and to negotiate a contract with any team. "After twelve years in the Major Leagues," Flood wrote, "I do not feel that I am a piece of property to be bought and sold irrespective of my wishes. I believe that any system which produces that result violates my basic rights as a citizen." Kuhn denied his request, and a year later, Flood filed a lawsuit challenging Major League Baseball's reserve clause. Although Flood lost his case, which reached the U.S. Supreme Court, his actions paved the way for the advent of free agency in baseball a few years later. ●

1960 Johnny Baker Post American Legion team

from the neighborhood play on the local diamonds were increasingly rare. Some African Americans were playing on integrated baseball and softball teams in Minneapolis and St. Paul rec leagues, but the all-black adult baseball teams in the Twin Cities were a thing of the past, and all-black fast-pitch softball teams were rapidly fading as well.

As discussed in the previous chapter, many talented young kids from the Rondo neighborhood played baseball in the Oxford house league. Only a few of them played baseball in high school, but they were among the best athletes around, participating in two, three, or more sports throughout the year.

Roger Neal was an outstanding athlete. He was skilled at baseball and also played football and basketball and ran track in high school. He was one of the fastest in the state in the 100-yard dash, a quick guard on the basketball team, and the halfback on the football team. He and I have remained friends ever since our playing days at Ober Boys Club in the 1950s. Roger's sons Leon Neal (Washington State) and Rashon Powers-Neal (Notre Dame) inherited their father's athleticism.

Brothers Larry and Bernie Buford were both unbelievable athletes. Their speed was especially amazing. Bernie was what one would call a four-tool player with his ability to field, throw, run, and hit for average; Larry also could hit for power, making him a five-tool guy. But the Buford brothers did not play baseball at Central High School. Bernie explained

The End of Rondo

IN THE 1930S, Rondo Avenue was at the heart of St. Paul's largest African American neighborhood. African American families who had been in Minnesota for decades mixed with newly arrived transplants from the South to form a vibrant community, one that was in many ways isolated from and independent of the white communities surrounding it. By the 1950s, an estimated 85 percent of St. Paul's African American population lived in Rondo's neighborhoods.

Soon, however, that central Rondo Avenue, and much of the community, was all but obliterated with the construction of Interstate 94. The freeway went right through the heart of Rondo, and hundreds of homes and businesses were destroyed. Thousands of African Americans were displaced and forced out into what was a racially segregated city with a discriminatory housing market. Although some black residents were able to stay in the area, the community was decimated.

My family lived at 409 St. Anthony at the time, and the homes across the street were removed to make room for the I-94 corridor. I would watch as the large construction graders literally changed the landscape of our community. City administrators had ignored recommendations from the federal government and environment reports that suggested that the desired path for Interstate 94 would be a route that ran north of University Avenue.

You can imagine the devastation to those who were displaced: no new homes available to absorb the change; people left to struggle without any support from the city. In addition, despite promises that the project would create employment opportunities for the current residents, even the general labor jobs were given to others.

In the summer of 2015, St. Paul Mayor Chris Coleman and Minnesota Commissioner of Transportation Charles Zelle acknowledged, belatedly, the travesty of the neighborhood's destruction. Zelle called it an "atrocity," while Coleman cited the "stain of racism that allowed so callous a decision as the one that led to families being dragged from their homes." Each offered apologies from their respective offices. "Today as mayor of St. Paul," Coleman said, "I apologize, on behalf of the city, to all who call Rondo home, for the acts and decisions that destroyed this once vibrant community." He declared July 17 "Rondo Remembrance and Reconciliation Day" in St. Paul. ●

that, although baseball was his favorite sport, their father, Melvin, wanted Larry and Bernie to star in football. Melvin Buford had been one of the first black students at Central, but he quit in order to join the Harlem Globetrotters. Another Buford brother, Mike, played football and earned all-city honors his junior year, but he quit high school and went into the military. Larry was the best athlete of the family, but he also could be lazy, according to Bernie—probably because everything came so easy to him. Bernie eventually took a job to help support the family, ending his sports career.

Another outstanding three-sport athlete, William "Wells" Price ran track at Marshall Junior High and then starred in football and basketball at Mechanic Arts High School. Only five foot nine, he could stand flat-footed under the basket and dunk a volleyball. Wells also joined the track team and ran the 100- and 220-yard dashes and anchored the 4 x 100 relay team. He accepted a football scholarship to Winona State College. Woody Larson, our pee wee and midget baseball coach, says he once told a scout from the Dodgers to stay in touch with Wells because of his baseball abilities. Unfortunately, Wells proved to be another example of a black baseball player from the Twin Cities who chose to pursue other sports as he got older. (It's also likely that the Dodgers rep didn't take Woody's advice, since many scouts didn't make African American players a priority, even after the success of Jackie Robinson, Willie Mays, and so many others.)

I played against Tom Hardy, and he was also a teammate of mine with the Giants in the Oxford house league. I can remember pitching to Tom in midget baseball and him blasting a home run or two off my fastballs, hitting them into the trees over the short rightfield fence. He played baseball, basketball, and football at Central High School and was an all-conference player in all three sports. Tom enrolled at the University of Minnesota at Duluth, where he opted for basketball over football, but his experience at UMD was not as enjoyable as he had hoped. The coaches urged him to take easier classes to ensure that he remained eligible. This advice didn't sit well with Tom, who had been a National Honor Society student in high school and was intent on earning a college education. The coaches won out, and Tom, disappointed in his class selection, transferred to Macalester College in St. Paul, where he would play two seasons of basketball. Tom had received baseball offers out of high school, but he had decided that basketball was the course he wanted to follow.

Another talented athlete, Ray Whitmore was an imposing player at the plate. In retrospect, he reminds me of Dave Winfield: tall and big and persuasive—if you're playing third base, you back up a few steps. I'm not sure why Ray didn't pursue baseball, but I tell you he could play.

The demographics of the high schools in both St. Paul and Minneapolis in the 1960s reflected what was seen in the larger society. Even at schools with relatively large numbers of African American students, the faculty and administrative personnel were overwhelmingly white. At Minneapolis's North High School in 1960, for example, among seventy-two individuals on the administrative and teaching staffs, only one was African American, a teacher. The lunch and maintenance staffs had no people of color among nineteen employees.

The extracurricular student activities reflected a similar skew. The choir at North included ninety-eight students and not one student of color. Among the seventy-nine members of the band were just three African Americans. There were six black students among the school's ninety-four boys who were letter winners in sports.

Looking back on my time at Mechanic Arts High School and Marshall Junior High School, I realize that the situation was very similar to that at Minneapolis North High School. I went to school to learn and didn't think much about who the staff members were, but in retrospect I recall that the vast majority of teachers, counselors, office staff, and custodians were not people of color.

Steve Sudduth graduated from North High School in 1966 and participated in four sports there: football, basketball, baseball, and track. North was fed by four or five parochial schools, and, according to Steve, by the time African Americans arrived to participate in sports, the coaches already had in mind who was going to be playing. During tryouts for football, the coach would direct players to certain positions, often ignoring the black students. Steve remembers that when he was asked where he had played prior to high school, his response of "Phyllis Wheatley" did not exactly get a positive reaction from the coach, even though some of the Wheatley teams had gone undefeated in baseball.

Steve, who would make the all-city team in both baseball and football, was the only African American on North's varsity baseball team in 1966. When the team didn't have games, he was told to participate on the varsity track team or else he would be flunked in physical education class, which would mean he couldn't graduate.

Steve recalls that many of his longtime friends, who he knew were gifted athletes, were denied the opportunity to play on the varsity team and became discouraged. Frank Davis, for example, had been a terrific shortstop but lost interest in baseball after the coach wouldn't put him into games. It was the same with Charles Howard, who also played three sports. Steve described Charles as an excellent athlete who could really jump: he was able to dunk two volleyballs at the same time.

Steve's younger brother, Lester, played on North's varsity baseball team for three years (1967–69) and later played football and baseball at Southwest Minnesota State College (now Southwest Minnesota State University) in Marshall. He was one of the first African American quarterbacks at Southwest State.

A few years older than the Sudduth brothers was John Washington, who played baseball at North High School from 1963 to 1965. He would go on to coach both baseball and basketball at Patrick Henry High School in North Minneapolis, and from 1996 to 2012 he served as the athletic director for Minneapolis Public Schools.

Another friend from the "other side of the river," Obie Kipper Jr., attended Washburn High School in South Minneapolis, a predominantly white school. He loved sports and played baseball, including on a championship American Legion team, but decades later he explained that he didn't try out for the baseball team in high school because he knew he wouldn't get a fair look from the coaches. He wasn't going to let them humiliate him by cutting him when he knew he was good enough to play.

Obie attended Washburn after his family moved into a home at Oakland Avenue and Forty-fifth Street in South Minneapolis—in violation of the unwritten rules, or "covenants," of the time prohibiting blacks from

1968 Minneapolis North High School baseball team yearbook photo, with Lester Sudduth (front row, fifth from left)

living south of Forty-second Street. Most landlords and realtors adhered to this rule, but Obie explained that his father had a white friend negotiate the purchase of the home on his behalf. Obie recalls that, within six months after his family moved in, about half the homes on the block went up for sale.

Like most others at the time, Obie played three sports, including baseball at Nicollet Park (now Rev. Dr. Martin Luther King Jr. Memorial Park), Powderhorn Park, and McRae Park, all located in South Minneapolis. Although he opted against trying out for the baseball team, Obie did play football and run track at Washburn. He earned all-city and all-state honors in track, and in 1966 he accepted a track scholarship to Mankato State University (now Minnesota State University, Mankato) in southern

Minnesota. He starred in football at Mankato State, and in 1990 he was inducted into the school's sports Hall of Fame.

Minneapolis's Central High School (which closed in 1982) was another hotbed of talent on the west side of the river during the 1960s. Among the school's top athletes in the middle of the decade was Louis Boone. Lou's family had moved to Minneapolis from Tennessee as part of the great migration of African Americans to the North. Lou played many sports at Central—football, basketball, baseball, and track—staying active in all seasons. He played baseball with park board teams and later with the Johnny Baker American Legion team. In high school, he made the all-city squads in basketball and baseball.

After high school, Lou attended St. Cloud State College on a basketball scholarship, and he excelled. Although he would have relished pursuing baseball as well, he was permitted to play only one sport. One of the attractions for Lou when he was recruited by St. Cloud was that the team was going to play basketball against Tennessee State University, a historically black college located in Nashville. Lou had fond memories of family trips to Tennessee during his youth. When the time came, however, Lou was not allowed to travel with the team and was left behind in St. Cloud. The coach never gave him a reason, but Lou knew that it was because of southern attitudes about African Americans participating in sports with white players.

Lou later played professional slow-pitch softball with a team called the Norsemen, which also included Steve Winfield and Jim Bowen, another African American player; my father, Louis White, was on the coaching staff. Lou recalls playing against former major league baseball players, including ex–New York Yankee Joe Pepitone, when he was with the Norsemen.

After his stint with the Norsemen came to an end, Lou applied to the Amateur Softball Association (ASA) to have his amateur status reinstated so that he could participate in the local softball leagues the organization governed. Lou's team would advance to the national championship tournament for Class AAA, the highest ASA class at the time. They lost their first game of the double-elimination tournament, and so they had to win about fourteen games in order to play for the championship. They got on a hot winning streak, and in the final game, to win the championship, Lou came to bat in the bottom of the seventh inning, with one out and one man on base and his team down by a run. He hit a two-run homer and his team won the championship—the first Minnesota squad to do so at this level.

Louis Boone's cousin Walt Whitmore was an outstanding pitcher and multisport athlete. As teammates on the Central High varsity team for three years, the cousins would hone their skills together during the summer months, playing pitch-out with a brick wall behind the school as their backstop. Walt made the all-city baseball team playing for Central and earned a baseball scholarship to Mankato State. According to Lou, Walt was a true tactician as a baseball pitcher. He worked hard at pitch location and was considered sneaky fast; he threw a slider and could place the ball

LEFT: *Louis Boone of Central High School, featured in a yearbook photo, 1965*
RIGHT: *Walt Whitmore of Central High School, featured in a yearbook photo, 1966*

1961 Minneapolis Central High School baseball team yearbook photo

wherever he wanted it. Walt's Mankato team won the Northern Intercollegiate Conference (NIC) championship in 1968 and went on to play in the NCAA Midwest Regional Tournament. Walt received some interest from scouts of the New York Mets, although in the end nothing developed.

Also on those Central High baseball teams of the mid-sixties was the power-hitting Carl Mabone. A smaller version of Willie Horton, the all-star slugger for the Detroit Tigers, Mabone was similarly an imposing player at the plate; he oozed power. In addition to his baseball honors, Mabone was named to the all-city team in football at Central, and he landed a football scholarship at Mankato State, where he had a solid career as a running back. Mabone played basketball in high school, too.

Central's Charles "Chuck" Ford was one of the best pitchers on the Minneapolis side of the river during the 1960s. He had a nasty curveball, one that was compared to that of Camilo Pascual of the Twins.

Paul Hatchet was a three-sport athlete for Central at this time. He, too, pursued football at the collegiate level, receiving a scholarship from North Dakota State University, where he was one of NDSU's greatest running backs and a two-time AP All-American.

Central High School had several top athletes earlier in the decade as well. Fred Herndon was a star pitcher for Minneapolis Central in 1960 and 1961, and he made the all-city team. Later in life, Fred became a well-respected official for high school and college basketball and baseball.

Another star hurler for the Central squad in the early sixties was Carl Rogan. Perhaps Carl's most amazing connection to black baseball is his grandfather: Hall of Famer Wilbur "Bullet Joe" Rogan. "Bullet Joe" pitched sixteen seasons with the Kansas City Monarchs before retiring in 1938 at the age of forty-four. Primarily a pitcher, Rogan was also one of the Negro Leagues' best hitters and served as the Monarchs manager for several years.

Bullet Joe's grandson Carl didn't quite reach those Hall of Fame heights, but he was one of the top local high school pitchers of his day. Carl recalls that, while pitching for his American Legion team, he once threw nine straight fastballs to start a game, all for strikes, and not one of the batters even managed to swing the bat. During his senior year pitching for Central, he hurled a no-hitter in the first game of the season; he remembers the opposing coach congratulating him after the game, then adding, "you didn't deserve it." Rogan injured his rotator cuff after that game and would never pitch again. He still made the all-city team that year.

Harry "Butch" Davis played three years on the varsity team and made the all-city team as an outfielder in 1963, his junior year. Butch's father was W. Harry Davis, an influential African American activist and civic leader in Minneapolis; his grandfather, Lee C. Davis, was a catcher with the Kansas City Monarchs and one of Minnesota's great black players during the 1920s and '30s. Butch also earned all-city honors in basketball and football at Central. He received a football

Butch Davis (right) of Central High School, featured in a yearbook photo, 1964

scholarship to the University of Minnesota but transferred to University of Minnesota, Duluth.

In looking back on their playing days in the 1960s, guys such as Boone and Kipper and Sudduth all commented on how they were never invited to clinics, tryouts, or camps where high school and Legion teams could get a better look at their skills. Scouts and recruiters often remarked that they didn't see young black kids playing baseball, but where were they looking?

Ben Mchie, who served as the manager for the Central High team, noted that he was "just too small to be an impact player" in high school. It turns out that he went on to play baseball at Long Beach State University in California—a school with a storied baseball history. I know of only a handful of African Americans from Minnesota who played baseball at the collegiate level. Clearly Mchie was in an elite class. He later founded and now serves as executive director of the African American Registry, a tremendously helpful online resource and database of information on African American history and heritage.

1961 Oxford Playground pee wee baseball team, featuring Dave and Steve Winfield (back row, fourth and fifth from left) and coach "Big Six" Carter (behind Steve)

Of course, of all the great African American ballplayers to come out of the Twin Cities in the 1960s—or perhaps ever—none stand out more than the Winfield Brothers, David and Steve. I first heard of them when, upon returning from my time in the service in 1967, my father said to me, "Hey, Panch, have you seen the Winfields play? Man, they're good baseball players!" Steve, Dave, and I would eventually become like family, almost brothers, in a relationship that continues to today.

Steve and I played baseball together for one season in the early 1970s, as his team needed a catcher. I was on a couple of fast-pitch softball teams at the time, and I would play baseball whenever I could. It was fun to compete in baseball again. Bill Peterson was the coach of the team, and it included other players who had been on the Attucks Brooks Legion teams, and many of them had played or were playing college baseball.

Steve and Dave's pursuit of baseball began early in the sixties, primarily because their cousin Tom Hardy played and it seemed like the top game. The Winfield boys would spend hours upon hours playing wherever they could, pretending to be different major leaguers, particularly from the Twins. They would play in the lot next to the church, they would play in the street, they would play at Oxford playground, a half block from their house on Carroll Avenue.

The Winfields began playing for Bob "Big Six" Carter at Oxford and then started their long relationship with coach Bill Peterson playing for the Oxford midget team. Bill would become more than just their coach; he was like a father figure to them. Most of all he was their baseball teacher and mentor, instilling not only fundamentals but also a deep understanding of the game and a strong work ethic.

Steve, being older, was the first Winfield to star on the diamond, and then Dave took over as the premier player. Under Peterson's tutelage and with some excellent teammates, their Attucks Brooks American Legion team won the state tournament in 1967 and 1968. In 1969, without Steve, the team didn't reach the championship.

Steve was recruited to walk on at the University of Minnesota by Jerry Kendall, assistant coach for Gopher baseball under the legendary Dick Siebert. During his first year at the university, Steve played on the freshman team and did well enough to earn the starting centerfield job. Steve would say that he was at the University of Minnesota to receive an education, with a small glimmer of a dream to play baseball at the highest level.

During the season, Steve had the opportunity to attend a black conference in Oakland, California. This period was one of tremendous awakening for African Americans, and many young black people were attending such conferences, where they explored the black experience in America and the contributions of African Americans throughout the nation's history. They were looking to shake up the status quo and to fight the con-

Bill Peterson

BILL PETERSON, a longtime coach and mentor, holds an important place in the legacy of Minnesota black baseball. Though white, he influenced many great players from the Rondo neighborhood and elsewhere in the Twin Cities. My first acquaintance with Bill was when he played on a team that my father coached for VFW baseball.

Bill also recalls playing for an all-black adult baseball team called the Hawks in the St. Paul City League. No Legion program would pick up players from Central High School, where Bill was a student, due to the regulations regarding eligibility and school enrollment numbers, so he looked elsewhere for a team to join during the summer. He says that his Hawks teammates played "shadow ball" during practices.

After graduating from high school at age sixteen, Bill joined the Marine Corps. During his service, Bill was scouted by the Boston Red Sox but was told that he needed to improve his fundamentals. After three years in the Marines, he attended the University of Minnesota, where he played baseball for coach Dick Siebert. He was especially influenced by Glen Gostic, a freshman and the assistant coach, who Bill says was a "baseball fundamentals guru."

Bill made the Gophers baseball team in his sophomore year, and he would suit up for home games but, as the third-string catcher, did not travel with the team for road games. This experience led him to pursue a part-time job as a coach at Oxford playground rather than a professional baseball career. The birth of his son Scott also weighed heavily in his decision.

Bill was first recruited to be a volunteer hockey coach at Oxford and then took a position on the staff in the spring of 1961, while still playing baseball at the university. He eventually took over as the Oxford baseball coach and mentored some talented players, including Steve and Dave Winfield and, later, Paul Molitor.

Bill coached the Attucks Brooks American Legion baseball team from 1965 to 1975, leading the team to state tournament championships in 1967 and '68; they played in the tournament in 1969 but did not three-peat. Attucks Brooks returned to the tournament again in 1973 and won the championship in 1974 with Molitor. Peterson also coached Molitor at Cretin High School from 1973 to 1975; the team won the state baseball tournament in 1973 and '74.

More than three decades later, in 2006, Peterson returned to his alma mater to coach the Central High School baseball team. In his one season there, Central won the City Conference Championship outright, something a Central team had not accomplished in seventy years.

Bill Peterson is a veritable legend in St. Paul baseball, and even today most parents want their children to learn the game from him. There is no

tinuing indignities of discrimination and inequality while uplifting the ideals of community pride and individual self-worth.

Steve's coaches, however, informed him that the team had a double-header the same weekend as the conference, and he needed to be available to play. Steve chose to attend the conference anyway. After he returned to Minnesota, the freshman team was scheduled to play St. Thomas, a Division III school in St. Paul where some of his former Attucks Brooks teammates were playing. Steve was not given the starting centerfield position, which he interpreted as retaliation for attending the conference.

1968 Attucks Brooks American Legion state champions, featuring Steve and Dave Winfield (back row, fourth and fifth from left)

better baseball teacher than Bill. He continues to work with the Midway Baseball league and the Minnesota Twins' RBI program. In 2010, with funding from the city of St. Paul, Midway Baseball, the Friends of St. Paul Baseball, and Major League Baseball, a new field at the Dunning Sports Complex was named Billy Peterson Field in his honor. Bill helps to take care of this magnificent field as a volunteer.

Bill's influence on baseball in Minnesota is exemplified by the many great players that had the pleasure of playing for him and by the many honors he has received, such as the Play Ball! Minnesota Terry Ryan Award (2007) and the annual bestowing of the William "Billy P" Peterson Friend of the Game award by the St. Paul Saints. He also has been inducted into the Minnesota Softball Hall of Fame, the Mancini Baseball Hall of Fame, the ASA National Softball Hall of Fame, and the St. Paul Central High School Sports Hall of Fame. But his support for and influence in baseball in the Rondo neighborhood and in St. Paul's African American community are perhaps his most important contributions to baseball in Minnesota. ●

Steve recalls that the freshman team didn't play many games and mostly practiced during that first season. Keeping his thoughts to baseball, he played and performed well in a collegiate summer baseball league. But when the 1969 fall baseball season rolled around, Steve walked away from the game, still feeling the sting from his freshman year experiences. He would say later, "I thought college was about learning and getting an education," but it seemed like he was being asked to put baseball first.

Meanwhile, during his senior year at St. Paul's Central High School in 1969, Dave was recruited to play baseball at the University of Minnesota. He was also in his first year playing basketball at Central, and although the team had several established stars, it was easy to see that this young player had incredible talent on the court. Gopher baseball assistant Jerry Kendall came to watch Dave play in a basketball game and was very impressed.

In his first year at the University of Minnesota, Dave played on a freshman basketball team that also included future NBA player Jim Brewer as well as Corky Taylor and Henry Goodes. The Gophers finished as the second-best freshman team in the Big Ten conference that year, its first one playing a Big Ten schedule. (The top team was from the University of Indiana, featuring George McGinnis and Joby Wright.)

Steve, Dave, and I became teammates in the intramural basketball league during the 1970 school year. Steve started the team, the "Soulful Strutters," and Dave joined after deciding to concentrate on grades rather than playing varsity basketball during his sophomore year. The Soulful Strutters won the intramural championship. The team was full of excellent athletes, including Walt Bowser, Craig Curry, and Michael Davis.

When Bill Musselman became the head coach of Gopher basketball in 1971, the Soulful Strutters were asked to play the freshman team in a scrimmage game. Dave, then a junior, so impressed assistant coach Jim Williams that he was asked to join the varsity team. The headlines read, "Dave Winfield discovered in the IM basketball program." It was a great story line, but of course Dave had played on the second-best freshman team in the Big Ten just two years earlier, so it wasn't much of a "discovery."

Musselman—who later coached at the pro level in the American Basketball Association and the National Basketball Association—called Dave the best rebounder he ever coached. The Gophers won the Big Ten Conference title in 1971–72 with Winfield, Brewer, Taylor, Keith Young, Bobby Nix, Clyde Turner, and Ron Behagen.

Dave remained a star on the basketball team in his senior year, and he continued as the headliner on the baseball team under Coach Siebert. He had been recruited as a pitcher, but for Peterson's Attucks Brooks Legion team he had also played shortstop or outfield—anywhere to keep his bat in the lineup. Dave asked Siebert about playing another position when he didn't pitch, but Siebert told him that they had other players; they didn't need him to play every day.

During the off-seasons in 1971 and '72, Dave played for the Alaska Goldpanners in a collegiate summer league. The league was a who's who of elite West Coast college baseball players. In the summer between his junior and senior seasons with the Gophers, Dave was named the most valuable player of the summer league after leading in home runs and runs batted in.

Each fall after returning from productive summers in the Alaskan league, Dave would ask Siebert to let him play every day. As Winfield continued to prove himself as one of the best amateur players in the country, Siebert relented, and Dave became an everyday player during his senior year, taking his position in the outfield when he wasn't on the mound. That season, Dave Winfield was selected as a first-team All-American after achieving a 9–1 record with a 2.74 earned run average and 109 strikeouts in 82 innings as a pitcher. At the plate, he batted .385 with 33 runs batted in in 130 at bats. He would go on to be named Most Outstanding Player of the 1973 College World Series. Dave struck out fourteen batters in a 1–0 complete-game shutout against the University of Oklahoma, and he struck out fifteen but earned a no-decision in Minnesota's 8–7 loss to the University of Southern California. Dave posted a combined 1.56 earned run average for the College World Series. In the two games he also batted .467 (7 for 15) with two runs batted in.

Another story that highlights Dave's rare gifts as an athlete happened when, after baseball practice one day, he walked by an intramural

Dave Winfield with the University of Minnesota Gophers

track and field competition in progress. He decided to try his hand at the high jump—just because. He won the event with a jump of six feet, six inches.

As his collegiate career was coming to a close, Dave Winfield was drafted by four different professional teams: the Minnesota Vikings of the National Football League (even though he never played organized football), the Atlanta Hawks of the National Basketball Association, the Utah Stars of the American Basketball Association, and of course the San Diego Padres of Major League Baseball.

Going straight from college to the Padres, without a stop in the minor leagues, Dave would spend twenty-two seasons in major league baseball—including two with his hometown Minnesota Twins. His major league accomplishments are the stuff of legends: twelve consecutive all-star selections, seven Gold Glove awards for fielding, six Silver Slugger awards for hitting, and induction into the National Baseball Hall of Fame.

While his physical abilities and superior athleticism are undeniable, Dave would tell you that it was the hard work he put into improving his hitting skills, the constant study of the game and of opposing pitchers, and the long hours of on-field practice and off-field training that allowed him to succeed at the highest levels of the sport.

Steve Winfield may always live in the shadow of his younger brother in the sports world, but he was no slouch on the diamond. I remember watching Steve play in the Class A State Tournament in 1979 at St. Cloud. Playing for the West St. Paul Americans, Steve got a base hit, and a man in the crowd yelled, "You're not as good as your brother!" On the next pitch, Steve stole second base, and he turned to look at the man. A few pitches later, Steve stole third base and again glanced at the heckler, who put his hands in the air as if to acknowledge, "Okay, you the man!" Steve also homered in the game and threw out a runner at the plate from centerfield to erase a potential go-ahead score. The Americans won the Class A championship.

Having seen Steve play baseball and softball over so many years, I know that he was at least the equal of many other local guys who played in college or the minors. Although he does not have a plaque in Cooperstown alongside his brother's, Steve Winfield was part of the inaugural class of inductees into the Class A Baseball Hall of Fame by the Minnesota Baseball Association.

I was once chatting with an assistant coach at a high school basketball game I was officiating, and he commented that it was too bad that Steve hadn't been able to make it in baseball. He added that although both Steve and Dave were "troublemakers," Dave was too good to keep away from the big leagues. This gentleman had been a baseball scout back then, and that was the information he had on the Winfield brothers. I was surprised to hear him describe Steve as a troublemaker and told him that I believed Steve was, in fact, a great role model for young African Americans in Minnesota. I asked where he had heard that description of Steve, and he said it was from when Steve was in college. It seems that this misinformation from Steve's college years—a label he earned while he sought to expand his educational opportunities—may have had a big part in derailing his chances to play at a higher level.

Steve Winfield at bat for the Steichen's baseball team, circa 1982. Steichen's played in St. Paul's Class AA league. Photo courtesy of the Winfield family

·8·
Extra Innings

BY THE 1970S, black baseball in Minnesota was a far cry from what it had been just twenty, let alone fifty, years earlier. After the long journey from early town teams and semipro clubs through barnstorming teams to integrated minor leagues and, finally, a major league franchise, young African American athletes in Minnesota were moving further and further away from a game that had once captured the passions of so many in the community. Despite the work of pioneers like Phil "Daddy" Reid, barnstorming heroes such as Walter Ball and Bobby Marshall, baseball legends on the rise like Roy Campanella and Willie Mays, and stars of the hometown Twins, from Mudcat Grant to Rod Carew, Minnesota's glory days of homegrown black baseball were becoming a distant memory.

Jackie Robinson's historic debut in 1947, ending the long-standing policy of segregation in organized baseball, was met with rejoicing and elation throughout African American communities and beyond. It was seen as a momentous opening of the door to future generations of black athletes who wanted to play baseball at the highest level. But it soon became clear that the door had opened only a crack, and opportunities would remain limited for many years to come. Team owners were reluctant to take away jobs from white players. Even as major league organizations signed players from the Negro Leagues, many were relegated to minor league affiliates, where their prime years were squandered without a chance to play on the main stage.

The integration of major league baseball also had the unintended consequence of reducing the number of opportunities for African American ballplayers overall. Local all-black teams and the organized Negro

163

Leagues alike were no longer able to sustain themselves once the barrier had been toppled and the top black athletes began pursuing the dream of playing in organized baseball. At the same time, opportunities at the collegiate and professional level continued to grow in other sports, such as basketball, football, and track, and many athletes opted to engage in those activities instead. Fewer and fewer black students in Minnesota were pursuing baseball, even at the high school level.

When Jackie Robinson retired after ten seasons in the major leagues, there were still three teams that had not signed any black players. According to research by Mark Armour and Daniel R. Levitt for the Society for American Baseball Research (SABR), African Americans made up about 1.7 percent of all major league players in 1950, a time when 10 percent of the nation's population was black. By 1960, just after the last holdout (the Boston Red Sox) signed its first black player (Pumpsie Green), the number of African Americans in the major leagues had increased to almost 9 percent, nearly equivalent to the percentage of the general population. The numbers continued to rise through the 1960s, and by 1975, according to Armour and Levitt, 18.5 percent of all major leaguers were black while the numbers in the general population stood at only between 11 and 12 percent. Over the next twenty years, the percentage of major leaguers who were African American ranged from 16 to a high of 18.7 percent (in 1981). Beginning in the mid-nineties, however, there was a steady decline. By 2000, fewer than 13 percent of major leaguers were black, the lowest ratio since 1965. It dipped under 10 percent in 2005, and in 2012, the final year of Armour and Levitt's research, African Americans accounted for just over 7 percent of major league players, roughly equivalent to the numbers in 1958.

Of course, this decline in percentages occurred as the number of Latino major leaguers saw its most dramatic increases. The peak, according to Armour and Levitt, was 2009, when 28.5 percent of all major league players were Latino.

Since the most recent expansion in 1998, Major League Baseball has had thirty franchises, nearly double the number of teams from when Jackie Robinson made his debut fifty years earlier. Even with the dramatic increase in the number of roster spots at the major league level, as well as a corresponding increase in the number of affiliated minor league clubs,

African Americans have seen their participation at the highest levels of pro baseball drop rather dramatically over the last thirty to forty years. That decline is also evident in local youth, high school, and semipro baseball leagues throughout Minnesota.

Reduced participation by blacks at the major league level also coincided with the rise of the National Basketball Association and the ascendance of megastars such as Julius Erving, Magic Johnson, and Michael Jordan. By 2015, approximately three-quarters of the players in the NBA were African American. The National Football League also has a much higher percentage of African American players, about two-thirds.

Growing up in the Twin Cities in the 1950s, my friends and I would play baseball at playgrounds and parks, in St. Paul and Minneapolis, until we went to high school. By that point, because very few colleges offered baseball scholarships to black athletes, our chances for playing sports at that level were better if we pursued football, basketball, or track and field. While most of us enjoyed playing baseball and the competition it brought, our thoughts were not of making it in the major leagues. Some of us may have dreamed of becoming the next Jackie Robinson or Roy Campanella or Willie Mays, but most of us knew that the likelihood of succeeding at that level was remote.

Even though it was not major league baseball, we had watched many of our fathers and men of their generation playing baseball at the high levels of the Negro Leagues or with barnstorming teams or semipro black teams. These teams provided opportunities for African Americans to play, compete, and even make some money—in some cases more money than they could make at their regular jobs. They could excel in front of large crowds, sometimes larger than those in organized baseball, and many were instantly recognized wherever they went in African American communities.

Nowadays, many fathers and mothers grew up pursuing basketball and the dream of playing at a high level. It has become the preferred sport in many African American communities, particularly in urban areas. The number of young black athletes entering college to play basketball (and football) is overwhelming, as is the number of players at the professional level. (I must give a proud grandpa shout-out and mention that this includes my grandson Royce White, who was Minnesota's Mr. Basketball

IN THE COURSE OF MY MANY YEARS playing, coaching, and officiating in sports, I have encountered many individuals who were both truly excellent athletes and extraordinary people. Alex Rowell was one such person.

I met Alex when we were teammates on the Pillsbury Kings basketball team, which was based in Minneapolis; we won the 1974 National Amateur Basketball Association championship and were runners-up in 1975. Alex was from the city of North Chicago, about thirty-five miles north of Chicago, where he was a star in football, basketball, and baseball.

In 1964, Alex began his collegiate career at Luther College in Decorah, Iowa. At Luther, he decided to pursue baseball and basketball. He made the varsity team in both sports for four years and was named to all-conference teams in both sports all four years; he was also a district All American in basketball and All American in baseball.

In 1968, Alex was drafted in the first round, sixteenth overall, by the Minnesota Twins. That year he played for the St. Cloud Rox. Among his teammates were three future major leaguers: Danny Thompson, Dave Goetz, and Jim Nettles. Alex was voted the top player on the Rox team.

The following season he moved up to the Twins' Class A affiliate in the Carolina League, the Red Springs Twins, and then to the Double-A Charlotte Hornets. While playing in North Carolina, Alex encountered firsthand many of the racial inequities of the South. When the Charlotte team broke spring training camp, the organization found lodging for the white players. The black players had to find housing for themselves.

In Red Springs, he and another black player rented a room from a preacher and his wife. Alex recalled that the home had no air conditioning, and during the day he spent a lot of time lying in the backseat of his car reading. He enjoyed going on the road because the team stayed in air-conditioned hotels.

The treatment of African Americans in the South was something new to Alex, and the experience dampened his enthusiasm for pursuing a professional baseball career. In order to supplement his minor league salary, Alex also worked as a teacher and coach at Gustavus Adolphus College in St. Peter, Minnesota, during the off-season. He decided that he did not want to give up that opportunity in exchange for the struggles he was encountering in North Carolina. Alex appeared in two games for the Hornets in 1970, and that was the end of his career in organized baseball. He was twenty-four years old.

That Alex was experiencing the indignities of Jim Crow, day in and day out, as late as 1970 only underscores how difficult it must have been for the players in the late 1940s through the '60s, before the Civil Rights Movement had succeeded in chipping away at some of the legal impediments to equality in the South. These men were driven by their desire to play baseball at the highest level, despite the obstacles of Jim Crow. Alex was very fortunate to have had other options available to him, which allowed him to move on to the next phase of his life.

Back in Minnesota, in addition to playing on amateur basketball teams, Alex also played amateur baseball and was a teammate of Steve Winfield on a West St. Paul team. The team often played at McMurray Field, near Lake Como in St. Paul. Steve shared a story that illustrates Alex's tremendous baseball skills.

The two fields of McMurray North and South were contained in a large open space that now houses a baseball field and a soccer field. It is set in a slight valley, surrounded on three sides by a large slope that bordered the leftfield area of both baseball fields. The fields were oriented opposite each other, with home plate for the south field in the southwest corner of the plot and the north field's plate in the northeast corner. The centerfielders from each field often found themselves standing next to each other, facing different directions.

Alex Rowell (standing, fourth from left) with the St. Cloud Rox, 1968. Myron Hall Collection, Stearns History Museum, St. Cloud, Minnesota

Steve recalled that, in different games, Alex hit home runs on both fields that landed at the bottom of the slope—more than five hundred feet away. Steve asserts that they were the longest hit balls he's ever seen in amateur baseball—and Steve, who played in that same league until he was sixty years old, has seen a lot of baseball games in his life.

Bill Peterson, who was the director of municipal athletics for St. Paul and was very familiar with the field, confirmed the distance. Bill also commented, "Alex hit the longest ball I've ever seen" at McMurray.

After giving up his dream of playing professional baseball, Alex and his wife, Saundra, went on to raise a family in St. Paul and built successful careers and lives for themselves. He is deeply involved in the community and, among other things, is a former high school and college basketball coach. ●

Sean McKamie

Sean McKamie at Vero Beach for Dodgers spring training, 1989

SEAN McKAMIE, who played baseball for St. Paul's Central High School from 1986 to '88, was the last (as of 2015) African American from St. Paul or Minneapolis to sign with a major league organization. McKamie was drafted by the Los Angeles Dodgers in the 1988 amateur baseball draft.

McKamie's baseball career began on a pee wee team at Dunning Field in St. Paul. He considered the coach, Jim Kelly, to be a second father. Sean remembers hanging out at Dunning until dark, playing baseball, football, or tennis. One of his early inspirations was Rod Carew: watching him play "made me love the game so much, and I would mimic his swing," said McKamie.

He continued to play at Dunning as he got older, joining the junior team coached by Rick Rangel. As a sophomore in high school, he went to a baseball clinic at the University of Minnesota, where coaches John

Anderson and Rob Fornasiere "loved me." McKamie played three years at Central High School. He was named to the all-conference team during his junior and senior years and was on the all-state team as a senior. Sean had a smooth glove and great hands, he could hit for average and for power, and he could run.

McKamie was drafted by the Dodgers in the twentieth round in June 1988. He signed with the organization for an $18,500 bonus, plus a guarantee that the team would pay for two years of college if he didn't make it in the pros. In February 1989, he was invited to extended spring training at Vero Beach, Florida. There he met John Roseboro, Willie Randolph, and Maury Wills, all of whom would have an influence on him. He remembers wanting to come home, but Randolph told him, "you have to work twice as hard, but you'll be okay."

During the 1989 season with the Dodgers' rookie team in the Gulf Coast League in Florida, he hit .316 and felt good about his performance. Then he damaged his rotator cuff and had to have surgery, which forced him to sit out the entire 1990 season. He came home to Minnesota for rehab.

McKamie returned to the field in 1991, with the Vero Beach Dodgers in Class A ball, and remained with the club for two more seasons, playing through injuries. He was assigned to the Bakersfield Dodgers in the High-A California League in 1993 and posted a .328 average in 21 games. McKamie seemed on the verge of moving up to Triple-A ball, but then he tore his hamstring (for the twelfth time).

He was back at Dodgers spring training in 1994 and was slated to go to Double-A ball, but he tore his hamstring again. The reinjury was devastating, and Sean decided that mentally he was done, even though the Dodgers wanted him to stay.

McKamie returned home to the Twin Cities to play for the Minneapolis Loons of the independent North Woods League. After two years with the Loons, he switched to the Southern Minny Stars of Austin, Minnesota, where he played in 1996 and 1997.

Sean admits that one of his biggest regrets was not staying with the Dodgers. "I'm not a quitter," he says, many years later. ●

in 2009 while playing at Hopkins High School and then was selected by the Houston Rockets as the sixteenth pick in the 2012 draft, after an outstanding one-year career at Iowa State.)

Even if parents want their child to play baseball, they cannot provide their own talents as baseball coaches since they don't have that experience. The baseball machine has become very expensive, as well. Young players are encouraged to attend showcases and to play on all-star traveling teams and in tournaments with the hope of being seen by scouts. These activities often require a significant financial commitment. With the greater opportunities for scholarships apparent in such sports as basketball and football, many families choose not to put their often limited financial resources toward developing a kid's baseball experience.

◆　◆　◆

I am entering my fifteenth year with the Minnesota Twins RBI—Reviving Baseball in Inner Cities—program. In partnership with the Minneapolis Park and Recreation Board and St. Paul Parks and Recreation, RBI seeks to provide more opportunities for city kids to play softball and baseball.

I can say that although we're having some success at getting young people of color to participate, the real challenge is retaining them into their high school years. We currently have more players of color participating in baseball and softball than we did forty years ago. We currently have six African American players on college baseball teams, something that hasn't happened in my lifetime.

So, how do we entice young kids to play baseball—a sport that is often tagged as boring and slow, or as "that white boy's sport"? There is no easy answer, but the staff at RBI continues to train and recruit young players and encourages parents to expose their children to baseball and softball. Baseball may not be as "cool" as basketball and football, but if you don't have a realistic chance of making it in those sports, baseball offers another opportunity.

If you talk with African Americans about baseball, there's not much of a conversation. The influence has long disappeared from the playgrounds at Oxford or Ober Boys Club, at Phyllis Wheatley and Sumner Field, and at old Nicollet Park (now Martin Luther King Park) in Minneapolis. Yes, there are a few players participating, and I hope that we can continue to recruit more, but it's the bottom of the ninth, there are two outs, the count is three and two, and the pitcher on the mound is the NBA or the NFL. It's time for folks to step up and revive black baseball in Minnesota.

Former ballplayers, Twins players and coaches, and youngsters from the Twins RBI program at the Metrodome for African American Heritage Night in 2006. Standing, left to right: coach Jerry White, John Cotton, Cecil Littles, Rondell White, Ken Christian, Shannon Stewart, LeRoy Hardeman, and Torii Hunter.

Appendix
They Passed Here Along the Way

African American and Latino Players on Minnesota's Minor League Clubs

N = Played in the Negro Leagues
M = Played in Major League Baseball
H = Inducted into the National Baseball Hall of Fame

ST. PAUL SAINTS, AMERICAN ASSOCIATION, 1948–60

Dan Bankhead, pitcher (N, M)	1948
Roy Campanella, catcher (N, M, H)	1948
Jim Pendleton, outfield/third base (N, M)	1949–51
Joe Black, pitcher (N, M)	1951
Edmundo "Sandy" Amoros, outfield (N, M)	1952
Bob Wilson, outfield/third base (N, M)	1952–53, '58
Charlie Neal, second base (N, M)	1954
Edward Moore, outfield	1954–55
Rene Valdes, pitcher (M)	1955
Solomon "Solly" Drake, outfield (M)	1956

ST. PAUL SAINTS, AMERICAN ASSOCIATION, 1948–60, *continued*

Granville Gladstone, outfield	1956–57
Lacey Curry, outfield/infield	1956–60
John Glenn, outfield (M)	1957–60
Felipe Montemayor, outfield/first base (M)	1958
Rene Friol, catcher	1958–59
Joe Caffie, outfield (M)	1959
Earl Robinson, outfield/third base (M)	1959
Guillermo "Willy" Miranda, shortstop (M)	1960
Fernando "Freddy" Rodriguez, pitcher (M)	1960

MINNEAPOLIS MILLERS, AMERICAN ASSOCIATION, 1949–60

Dave Barnhill, pitcher (N, H)	1949–51
Ray Dandridge, third base (N)	1949–52
Willie Mays, outfield (N, M, H)	1951
Artie Wilson, outfield (N, M)	1951
Hank Thompson, outfield (N, M)	1951, '57
Ray Noble, catcher (N, M)	1953
Amado Ibanex, pitcher	1953–55
Fernando Osorio, pitcher	1954
Ramon Monzant, pitcher (M)	1954–56
Monte Irvin, outfield (N, M, H)	1955
Lou Ortiz, second base	1955
Willie Kirkland, outfield (M)	1955–56
Valmy Thomas, catcher (M)	1956
Ozzie Virgil, third base (M)	1956
Bill White, outfield (M)	1956
Fernando "Freddy" Rodriguez, pitcher (M)	1956–57
Felipe Alou, outfield (M)	1957
Orlando Cepeda, outfield (M, H)	1957

Webbo Clarke, pitcher (N, M)	1957
Carlos Paula, outfield (M)	1957
Bobby Prescott, outfield/third base (M)	1957
Andre Rodgers, shortstop (M)	1957
Jose Valdivielso, shortstop (M)	1958
Elijah "Pumpsie" Green, outfield (M)	1958–59
Earl Wilson, pitcher (M)	1959–60

ST. CLOUD ROX, NORTHERN LEAGUE, 1953–1968

John Kennedy, infield (N, M)	1953
Ozzie Virgil, infield (M)	1953
Willie Kirkland, outfield (M)	1954
Andre Rodgers, infield (M)	1955
Tony Taylor, infield (M)	1955
Leon Wagner, outfield (M)	1955
Orlando Cepeda, outfield (M, H)	1956
William DeJesus, pitcher	1956
Inocencio Rodriguez, outfield/infield	1956
Matty Alou, outfield (M)	1958
Harvey Branch, pitcher (M)	1960
Gil Carter, outfield	1960
Gene Petty, infield	1960–61
Lou Brock, outfield (M, H)	1961
Hal Gilson, pitcher (M)	1961–62
Bobby Brooks, outfield (M)	1965
Nathaniel King, infield	1965
Alex Rowell, outfield	1968

The 1972 pee wee city champions, from Oxford Playground, with coach Steve Winfield (back, center). This was St. Paul's last all-black pee wee baseball team. Standing at the far left is Scott Peterson, son of coach Bill Peterson (not pictured).

Sources and Bibliography

MY RESEARCH BEGAN with my personal experience watching my father and others play baseball for the Twin City Colored Giants and softball for the Ted Bies Liquor team, with playing baseball myself from age eight through adulthood, and with working at the Oxford Recreation Center during the late 1960s and early '70s. Most of my more recent research from newspapers and private papers was conducted at the Gale Family Library at the Minnesota Historical Society's Minnesota History Center in St. Paul.

Oral Interviews by the Author

Dr. Jim Allen, Woodbury, 2013

Marvin Anderson, St. Paul, 2013

Bob Bartholemew, Austin, Minnesota, 2012

Dennis Bartholemew, Maplewood, 2012

Julio Becquer, Minneapolis, 2010, 2011

Verlene Price Booker, St. Paul, 2012, 2014, 2015

Louis Boone, Minneapolis, 2014

Larry "Bubba" Brown, Minneapolis, 2010, 2011

Bernie Buford, Minneapolis, 2012

Ken Christian, St. Paul, 2009

Billy Collins, St. Paul, 2010

Ed Cotton, St. Paul, 2010, 2011

John Cotton, St. Paul, 2009

Lacey Curry Sr., Chicago, 2010, 2012

Harry "Butch" Davis Jr., Minneapolis, 2009

Sylvester Davis, Roseville, 2012, 2013, 2014

Lyle Gerhardt, Lakeville, 2011, 2013, 2014

Tom Hardy, Washington, DC, 2011, 2012

Ronnie Henderson, Minneapolis, 2005

Victoria Hopwood, Roseville, 2009

Rev. John Hunter, Minneapolis, 2012, 2013

Bob Karns, St. Cloud, 2008

Bob Kendrick, Kansas City, Missouri, 2004, 2009–2014

Obie Kipper Jr., Minneapolis, 2012, 2014, 2015

Gordy Kirk, St. Paul, 2013–2015

Woody Larson, Roseville, 2009–2011

Cecil Littles, St. Paul, 2009

Mary Littles, St. Paul, 2010, 2012

Kwame McDonald, St. Paul, 2004–2008

Benjamin Mchie, African American Registry, 2011

Sean McKamie, St. Paul, 2012, 2014

Yusef Mgeni, St. Paul, 2010, 2011, 2014, 2015

James Milsap, St. Paul, 2009, 2010

Roger Neal Jr., Maplewood, 2009, 2010, 2012, 2013, 2015

Buck O'Neil, Kansas City, Missouri, 2004

Tony Oliva, Bloomington, 2009, 2010

Armand Peterson, Minneapolis, 2010, 2014

Bill Peterson, St. Paul, 2009, 2015

Todd Peterson, Kansas City, Missouri, 2014

Lorna Livingston Pettis, Minneapolis, 2010

Gloria Presley-Massey, St. Paul, 2012, 2014

Norm "Speed" Rawlings, St. Paul, 2009, 2010, 2012–2015

Joe Ray, St. Paul, 2014, 2015

Paul Ray, St. Paul, 2013

Jim Robinson, St. Paul, 1987, 2009, 2010, 2015

Alex Rowell, Eden Prairie, 2014, 2015

Bob Rynda, Minneapolis, 2013–2015

Skip Schultz, Eden Prairie, 2009

Richard Selbitcska, Woodbury, 2012, 2013

Ozzie Virgil Sr., Dominican Republic (via Skype), 2014

Bill Walton, Oakland, California, 2011, 2012

Louis "Pud" White Jr., St. Paul, 1955, 2004

John Wilkes, Minneapolis, 2013, 2014

Pauline Williams, St. Paul, 2009–2012

Dave Winfield, St. Paul, 1970–2015

Steve Winfield, St. Paul, 1968–2015

Newspapers

The Appeal, February 23–September 28, 1889; June 12, 1897–October 19, 1912

Globe News, March 28, 1900; March 18, 1903; September 1, 1903

Minneapolis Messenger, May 7, 1921–March 10, 1923

Minneapolis Spokesman, August 10, 1934–July 14, 1939; January 12, 1940–July 29, 1949; February 3, 1950–August 29, 1958

Minneapolis Tribune, May 1–August 26, 1935

National Advocate, September 3, 1921–June 29, 1923

North West Umpires Review, June 4–August 13, 1950

Northwestern Bulletin, March 23, 1922–August 15, 1925

St. Paul Dispatch, 1944–1946

St. Paul Echo, November 7, 1925–October 16, 1926

St. Paul Pioneer Press, April 1–30, 1944

St. Paul Recorder, January 7, 1944–August 26, 1949

Twin City Herald, April 2, 1932–August 11, 1934; July 4–August 29, 1936; July 8 and 15, 1939; July 13, 1940

Twin City Leader, July 20–December 1940

Twin City Star, June 2, 1910–October 31, 1914

The Western Appeal, June 13, 1885–December 29, 1888

Books and Magazines

Britts, Maurice W. *Billy Williams: Minnesota's Assistant Governor.* St. Cloud, MN: North Star Press, 1977.

Cavett, Kate (as told to). *Voices of Rondo: Oral Histories of Saint Paul's Historic Black Community.* Minneapolis: Syren Book Company, 2005.

Coalition for the History of African American Contributions to the University of Minnesota. "Young, Gifted, and Black: Ninety Years of Experience and Perceptions of African American Students at the University of Minnesota, 1882–1972."

Dunkel, Tom. *Color Blind: The Forgotten Team That Broke Baseball's Color Line.* New York: Grove Press, 2013.

Grant, Jim "Mudcat," with Tom Sabellico and Pat O'Brien. *The Black Aces: Baseball's Only African American Twenty-Game Winners.* Chula Vista, CA: Aventine Press, 2007.

Griffin, James S. "Blacks in the St. Paul Police Department: An Eighty-Year Survey." *Minnesota History* (Fall 1975): 255–65.

Griffin, Jimmy, with Kwame JC McDonald. *Jimmy Griffin: A Son of Rondo: A Memoir.* St. Paul, MN: Ramsey County Historical Society, 2001.

Historical Collector's Edition. *Jackie Robinson: More than a Baseball Player—A Hero* 1 (2013).

Hoffbeck, Steven R. *Swinging for the Fences: Black Baseball in Minnesota.* St. Paul: Minnesota Historical Society Press, 2005.

James, Bill. *The New Bill James Historical Baseball Abstract.* Revised edition. New York: Free Press, 2003.

Jensen, Don. *The Timeline History of Baseball.* San Diego: Thunder Bay Press, 2009.

McKissack, Patricia C., and Fredrick McKissack Jr. *Black Diamond: The Story of the Negro Baseball Leagues.* New York: Scholastic, 1994.

Nelson, Paul D. *Fredrick L. McGhee: A Life on the Color Line, 1861–1912.* St. Paul: Minnesota Historical Society Press, 2002.

O'Neil, Buck, with Steve Wulf and David Conrads. *I Was Right on Time: My Journey from the Negro Leagues to the Majors.* New York: Fireside, 1996.

Peterson, Armand, and Tom Tomashek. *Town Ball: The Glory Days of Minnesota Amateur Baseball*. Minneapolis: University of Minnesota Press, 2006.

Peterson, Robert. *Only the Ball Was White: A History of Legendary Black Players and All-Black Professional Teams*. New York and Oxford: Oxford University Press, 1970, 1992.

Peterson, Todd. *Early Black Baseball in Minnesota: The St. Paul Gophers, Minneapolis Keystones and Other Barnstorming Teams of the Deadball Era*. Jefferson, NC: McFarland & Company, 2010.

Posnanski, Joe. *The Soul of Baseball: A Road Trip Through Buck O'Neil's America*. New York: William Morrow, 2007.

Ring, Jennifer. *Stolen Bases: Why American Girls Don't Play Baseball*. Champaign: University of Illinois Press, 2009, 2013.

Swanton, Barry, and Jay-dell Mah. *Black Baseball Players in Canada: A Biographical Dictionary, 1881–1960*. Jefferson, NC: McFarland & Company, 2009.

Taylor, David V. "John Quincy Adams: St. Paul Editor and Black Leader." *Minnesota History* (Winter 1973): 283–96.

Thornley, Stew. *Baseball in Minnesota: The Definitive History*. St. Paul: Minnesota Historical Society Press, 2006.

Tye, Larry. *Satchel: The Life and Times of an American Legend*. New York: Random House, 2008.

Tygiel, Jules. *Baseball's Great Experiment: Jackie Robinson and His Legacy*. New York and Oxford: Oxford University Press, 1983, 1997.

Online Articles and Resources

African American Registry, http://www.aaregistry.org/

Baseball-Reference.com

Basketball-Reference.com

BlackPast.org

The Donaldson Network, http://johndonaldson.bravehost.com/index.html

Goldman, Steven. "Segregated Baseball: A Kaleidoscopic Review." Major

League Baseball official website, http://mlb.mlb.com/mlb/history /mlb_negro_leagues_story.jsp?story=kaleidoscopic.

Hendricks, Henry. "St. Paul's Pilgrim Baptist Church Celebrates 150 Years." Twin Cities Daily Planet, June 29, 2013, http://www.tcdaily planet.net/give-grace-humble-150-years-pilgrim-baptist-church -celebration/.

"The History of Keokuk Web Site," http://www.keokuk.net/history/

Kansas State University, "A Look at Life in the Negro Leagues," http:// coe.k-state.edu/annex/nlbm/

Library of Congress, "Chronicling America: Historic American Newspapers," http://chroniclingamerica.loc.gov/

McClure, Jane. "Rondo Neighborhood." *Saint Paul Historical*, http://saint paulhistorical.com/items/show/160.

Minnesota Historical Society, Collections Online, http://search.mnhs. org/

Minnesota Historical Society, Digital Newspapers at MNHS, http:// www.mnhs.org/newspapers

MLB.com, "Negro Leagues Legacy," Major League Baseball official website, http://mlb.mlb.com/mlb/history/mlb_negro_leagues.jsp

MNopedia.org

Muchlinski, Alan, and David Muchlinski. "The Pipestone Black Sox." http://instructional1.calstatela.edu/amuchli/pipestone.htm.

National Baseball Hall of Fame and Library official website, http://base-ballhall.org/

Negro League Baseball.com, http://www.negroleaguebaseball.com/

Negro League Baseball Players Association, http://www.nlbpa.com/

Negro Leagues Baseball eMuseum, https://www.coe.ksu.edu/annex /nlbemuseum/

Negro Leagues Baseball Museum official website, https://www.nlbm .com/

Pitch Black Negro League Site, http://www.pitchblackbaseball.com

Spangler, Earl. "The Negro in Minnesota, 1800–1865." Manitoba Historical Society official website, http://www.mhs.mb.ca/docs/transactions /3/negroinminnesota.shtml.

Thornley, Stew. "Minnesota Baseball History." Minnesota Twins official website, http://minnesota.twins.mlb.com/min/history/minnesota _baseball_history.jsp.

Thornley, Stew. "Twin Cities Ballparks." http://stewthornley.net/twin cityballparks.html.

Videos and Documentaries

Burns, Ken, writer, producer, and director. *Baseball*. Walpole, NH: Florentine Films and the Baseball Project, 1994, 2001.

Davidson, Craig, producer and director. *There Was Always Sun Shining Someplace: Life in the Negro Baseball Leagues*. Narrated by James Earl Jones. Westport, CT: Refocus Films, 1981, 2007.

MLB Network. *Pride & Perseverance: The Story of the Negro Leagues*. Narrated by Dave Winfield. New York: Major League Baseball Productions, 2009.

Negro Leagues Baseball Museum. *Discover Greatness: An Illustrated History of Negro Leagues Baseball*. Kansas City, MO: Negro Leagues Baseball Museum, 1993.

Negro Leagues Baseball Museum. *They Were All Stars: An Historic Narrative of Negro Leagues Baseball*. Narrated by James Earl Jones. Kansas City, MO: Negro Leagues Baseball Museum.

O'Neil, Buck, and Louis White. Interview by Kwame McDonald. Negro Leagues Baseball Museum, 2004.

Organizations and Museums

Dakota County Historical Society, South St. Paul

Dunn County Historical Society, Menomonie, Wisconsin

George Latimer Central Library, Special Collections, St. Paul

History Theatre, St. Paul

Minneapolis Central Library, Minneapolis History Collections and Special Collections, Minneapolis

Minneapolis Park and Recreation Board, Minneapolis

Minnesota Amateur Baseball Hall of Fame, St. Cloud Civic Center, St. Cloud, Minnesota

Minnesota Twins Baseball Team, Target Field, Minneapolis

Negro Leagues Baseball Museum, Kansas City, Missouri

Ramsey County Historical Society, St. Paul

St. Peter Claver Catholic Church, St. Paul

Stearns History Museum, St. Cloud, Minnesota

Index

Page numbers in *italic* type indicate illustrations.

They Played for the Love of the Game was designed and set in type by Judy Gilats in St. Paul, Minnesota. The text face is Alda and the display face is SantElia Rough. The book was printed at Sheridan Books, Chelsea, Michigan.

CPSIA information can be obtained
at www.ICGtesting.com
Printed in the USA
JSHW030833081221
21056JS00001B/2